F

Essays On India, America,
And The In-Between

Sayantani Dasgupta

Two Sylvias Press

Two Sylvias Press
PO Box 1524
Kingston, WA 98346
twosylviaspress@gmail.com

Cover Art: *Untelling* by Abhishek Chaudhary
(www.rangeenmakhee.tumblr.com)
Cover Design: Kelli Russell Agodon
Book Design: Annette Spaulding-Convy
Author Photo Credit (back cover): Heather Woolery
(www.heatherwoolery.com)
Author Photo Credit (interior): Amrinder Singh Grewal

Created with the belief that *great writing is good for the world*, Two Sylvias Press mixes modern technology, classic style, and literary intellect with an eco-friendly heart. We draw our inspiration from the poetic literary talent of Sylvia Plath and the editorial business sense of Sylvia Beach. We are an independent press dedicated to publishing the exceptional voices of writers.

For more information about Two Sylvias Press or to learn more about the eBook version of *Fire Girl* please visit: www.twosylviaspress.com

First Edition. Created in the United States of America.

ISBN: 13: 978-0692721254
ISBN: 10: 0692721258

Two Sylvias Press
www.twosylviaspress.com

Praise For *Fire Girl*

These are exquisite essays, filled with savory language spiced just right. Sayantani Dasgupta's generous intelligence and lively curiosity bring alive whole worlds—those of ancient stories and those of daily living, artfully considered. Cultures, languages, religions, landscapes, legacies—this is a writer who contains multitudes.
—Peggy Shumaker, Author of *Just Breathe Normally*

80

Sayantani Dasgupta writes with such keen intelligence and vivid clarity that we can't help be taken in. Lyrical, compassionate, and compelling, these beautiful essays transport us to another world. In Dasgupta's able hands, it is a world we come to recognize as our own.
—Kim Barnes, Author of *In the Kingdom of Men*

80

Sayantani Dasgupta brings together past and present as she considers childhood, violence, safety, family, monsters, goddesses, and the concept of home. These beautiful essays move between India and America, between selves and versions of selves, as Sayantani considers what is real and what is story or indeed, how the two are ever different. The range of landscapes and subjects is as breathtaking as the writing, showing us a powerful mind at work.
—Bich Minh Nguyen, Author of *Stealing Buddha's Dinner*

80

The oscillations in the essays are sometimes gentle vibrations, other times beating drums, encompassing the

tension between the home and the world, the past and the present, the brain and the heart. The stories constantly go away and come back and we undulate with them, rippling between delight, sorrow, rage, wonder.
—Aurvi Sharma, Winner of the *2015 Gulf Coast Prize in Nonfiction*

Acknowledgements

Thanks to the following journals and magazines for first publishing some of the essays included in this collection:

- *The Rumpus:* "Goddesses"
- *Phoebe:* "Oscillation"
- *The Toast:* "Why Home is a Bad Bollywood Movie"
- *Gulf Stream:* "Fire Girl"
- *SN Review:* "On Seeking Answers"
- *Conversations Across Borders:* "Touching Down" (the first section of "In the Land of Water")
- *Yellow Medicine Review:* "On Collecting Stories"
- *Idaho Magazine:* "Beyond the Ivory Tower"
- *The Drunken Odyssey Podcast:* "On Loving Captain Nemo"

And in the same breath, big thanks to my friend Jordan Hartt for saying, "Hey, why not put them all together in one book?"

Shout-out to my teachers—Ron McFarland and Joy Passanante—and especially Kim Barnes for infinite lessons on writing, courage, vulnerability, and life. Thanks also to writers extraordinaire—Peggy Shumaker, Bich Minh Nguyen, and Aurvi Sharma—for their friendship.

I am grateful to my friends—Subhadip Purakayastha, Suvena Bansal, Manasi Kanuga, Rohit Talwar, Parul Pal, Annie Lampman, Brandon Schrand, Kelli Schrand, Brittney Carman, Jamaica Ritcher, Jill Kellogg-Serna, Jeff Jones, Kelly Roberts, Rochelle Smith, Michael Filipowski, Sunaina Mathur Dalaya, Smita Naha, and Rajarshi Sengupta. Thank you for being such towering pillars of support, for your words, many good meals, and raging discussions about and against the rest of the world.

My deepest appreciation for Kelli Russell Agodon and Annette Spaulding-Convy of Two Sylvias Press for believing in *Fire Girl* and for bringing her to the world.

The first storytellers in my life came in the form of family members—my grandfather and best friend Asit Ranjan Dasgupta, my paternal and maternal grandmothers Minati and Chhaya Dasgupta, and my aunt and uncle, Nabanipa and Saumyabrata Sengupta. They filled my life with uncountable gifts and immeasurable affection. My first audience was my brother Aritro, whose demand for stories kept me on my toes. To Sinjini, my little sister, a tight hug and kiss. To Partha and the rest of my family in Bangladesh, thank you for your warmth and wonderfulness. To my husband, Amrinder Singh Grewal, thanks for being my good luck charm, my staunchest advocate, and my champion reader.

And finally, a thousand thanks to my parents, Atanu and Swapna Dasgupta, for being the most encouraging voices in my life from the moment I wrote my first story (a curious blend of *Cinderella* and *Snow White*, written in red ink and in Hindi) right down to this day. Without your love, support, and blessings, none of this would ever have been possible.

Table of Contents

For my parents, Swapna & Atanu Dasgupta

"Still there are times I am bewildered by each mile I have traveled, each meal I have eaten, each person I have known, each room in which I have slept. As ordinary as it all appears, there are times when it is beyond my imagination."

—Jhumpa Lahiri, *Interpreter of Maladies*

Reptilian Brain

The year I turned twenty I was hired for my first internship. Armed with a recently-acquired BA degree in history, I was waiting to hear back from two universities I had applied to for masters' programs. In the meanwhile, I answered an ad for a human resources intern at a software company and after a half hour interview, was told I had the job. I cannot overstate how successful that made me feel. I was a grown woman and a graduate of St. Stephen's College, one of India's premier educational institutions. I was old enough to vote, to marry, to acquire a job, and hopefully hold it down. "Bring it," I egged the world.

I still remember that it was a Tuesday morning. Devout Hindus in North India dedicate Tuesdays to the worship of Hanuman, the monkey god. Prayers are offered at temples and shrines built in his honor. Many eat only one meal and forgo the rest. In my family, we did neither. Worshipping a monkey, no matter how much his presence and power were justified by mythology, seemed farfetched.

I dressed with care, indigo and black salwar kameez, black high heels. But the fabric didn't breathe. It wasn't cotton. It was some synthetic, going-to-make-you-sweat-but-you-are-stuck-with-it material, and at age twenty, I should have known better because the sky that morning was an angry orange net stretched tight across the blue expanse. There was no breeze and combined with New Delhi's notorious pollution, the air was hard to breathe. The city smoldered, for it was June, and under that hot sun, we were no different from the pale corncobs that vendors spiced with lemon juice and roasted in the temporary shacks they built on the sidewalks.

My office sat in the basement of a grey building. Because of its location as well as its powerful air-conditioning, it was paradise compared to the scorching world outside. As I boarded the first of the two buses that would take me to my destination, I thought longingly of my cubicle, my hole in the ground, cool and safe.

There were no empty seats inside the bus. Passengers stood in congested, assembly-line formats, and the unluckiest of the men who couldn't be stuffed inside, hung precariously from the sidebars at the door. I feared for these men. One abrupt brake, one lost foothold, one grip slipping off the handle, and the effects could range from a bag sliding off a shoulder to a bone-muscle-sinew crunching end under the wheels. I feared for them, yes, but not too much, because they were the same nameless, faceless, touchy-feely kind of men who ran amok in New Delhi. They took advantage of its crowds to make kissing sounds and to sneak in nimble fingers to pinch a hip or flick an unsuspecting nipple.

By the time I got off at my first destination, Savitri Cinema, my salwar kameez was stuck to my back. I cursed my clothing choice and thought longingly of my cubicle. "Just a few more minutes," I consoled myself.

It was then that I noticed the man across the street.

&

The Reptilian Brain sits at the base of our skull and connects to both the spinal column and the cerebellum. It is the oldest and smallest component of the human brain and is like the entire brain of present day reptiles. Evolutionarily speaking, it developed millions of years ago, and while it is the most ancient and primitive part of us, it is also the most advanced. It is the first to develop within a growing fetus, and throughout an individual's life, it remains responsible for survival functions, such as motor behavior, respiration, and reproduction. Eerily enough, it continues to live on when someone is brain dead, and conversely, when the Reptilian Brain dies, so does the rest of the body.

ॐ

The man was dressed in ochre clothes, the preferred garb of Hindu holy men all over the country. He was of moderate height, skinny but tightly muscled. In the most ordinary of circumstances, I would never have noticed him, for he was another ordinary man on the streets of New Delhi. But that morning, he was unmissable. And in my indigo and black salwar kameez, gleaming under the orange sun, so was I.

At first, I thought it was a scarf around his neck. Surely, only an idiot would wear one as thick and heavy as a human arm on a hot, New Delhi, June morning. From where I watched, it slithered slowly, unmistakably corn-yellow, round and round the man's neck, and brought its triangular flat head towards my world.

I inhaled sharply. The earth had stopped spinning.

I didn't know then, but in a matter of minutes, I was going to be forced to memorize the narrow-pinchedness of his face and his sharp moustache, etched like a line over his thin lips.

ॐ

There are nearly 3,500 species of snakes in the world, and they can be found on every continent except

Antarctica. They are ectothermic or "cold-blooded." They have one functional lung. They lay their eggs on land and possess neither eyelids nor external ears. The word "snake" comes from the Proto-Indo-European "sneg," which means "to crawl," and "serpent" comes from "serp" or "to creep." India has a few hundred odd varieties of snakes, of which four are poisonous. The rest are assets. They keep the rodent population under control and some are, in fact, so tame you can wear them around your wrist like bracelets.

I grew up fascinated with snakes, with facts such as these on my fingertips. But the reality of living in a city like New Delhi meant that I had very little to actually do with snakes, my interactions limited to watching them on TV or inside glass cages in zoos. My family never owned pets and neither did any of my friends nor anyone in my extended family. A house snake was completely out of the question. But I read, I researched, I watched every relevant documentary that National Geographic and Discovery Channel produced. Every time I read a headline on snake poaching or killing because some illiterate villagers or stupid urbanites had decided to get rid of their local snake population, I frothed with indignation. Once in the seventh grade, when our school arranged for a class trip to the zoo and a few of my classmates shrieked at the sight of a python resting inside a glass room, I laughed unkindly. I saw no reason why their fear should not be the target of my mockery.

What was the allure of snakes in my mind? I wonder how much of my fascination had to do with the adolescent need to appear cool and different than everybody else. What else would explain my armchair activism? I don't remember falling in love with their shine or symmetry. It wasn't the quickness of their movements. Nor the grace nor simplicity of their design or anatomical construction. I was fascinated by snakes because, for so many girls my age, they were a source of fear. I didn't realize then that textual knowledge, no matter how accurate and detailed, is a poor substitute for real life.

∞

On any given day, the streets in and around New Delhi's Savitri Cinema crawl with traffic and people and the occasional wildlife in the form of cows, cats, and stray dogs. It snarls with busyness, with only minimal room left for niceties and courtesies. Most days, its residents—both descendants of the city's original settlers as well as the several million who have migrated here from other parts of India in addition to the rest of South Asia—get by on a precarious combination of fortune and fortitude. Some days, they might even blaze through. On her maiden visit to New Delhi, Tina Turner is believed to have said, "There were so many people, and oh, the traffic." The city's own sons, such as the novelist Khushwant Singh, have lamented, "In Delhi, death and drink make life worth living." Is it an improbable birthplace for poets and philosophers? Or perhaps it *is* the chaos that fuels their stillness.

I crossed the street with one eye firmly on the man and his thick yellow scarf. His gaze shifted from one direction to another, measuring, squinting at the ocean of faces. He was, as I soon learned, hunting.

I walked with as much speed as high-heeled shoes will allow any woman. I averted my eyes, kept them glued to my feet, and bypassed him, the voice inside my head euphoric that I hadn't been spotted. But my indigo-black salwar kameez gave me away, and I heard his voice call out, "Madam, wait." I didn't have to turn around to know he meant me.

ॐ

The Reptilian Brain is responsible for xenophobia, rage, territoriality, social hierarchy, and the desire to submit to stronger members of one's own species. It constantly tests incoming stimuli from the environment for indication of threat. Once danger is detected, the body is put on high alert, and the hormone adrenaline decides which option to exercise between flight or fight. Irrespective of this decision, the body shifts into a realm of altered time. The victim's metabolism speeds up, but because the responses of the Reptilian Brain are faster than the human body's normal state of consciousness, she *feels* everything has slowed down. It overrides the more rational impulses of the brain and results in unpredictable primitive behavior. The actions of the Reptilian Brain are purely instinctual, which explains why market researchers have increasingly grown attentive to it in order to understand what a product can do for the consumer at the most fundamental level.

ॐ

Like an obedient student or disciple, his command rooted me to my spot. Why? Is the need to please inbuilt in women? Was I afraid to seem impolite? Or rude? Why didn't I ignore his order and just keep walking?

He joined me in a couple of strides. He was not

alone. Two more men appeared out of the dry heat of the city. They, too, wore snakes like necklaces. Brothers. They formed a circle around me, the snakes lengthening and shortening. Six pairs of icy eyes. One girl with frightened skin.

The leader asked, "Madam, are you a student?"

"Yes." Words tumbled out of my mouth as if I had lost all ability to rein them in, "I am a student. No, I *was* a student. No, no, I *am* still a student. I suppose. I am waiting for my final results. And I am working. As an intern. But it's temporary. Once I get my results, I will go back to being a student."

"So you are waiting for your results?" He repeated slowly.

"Yes."

His thin lips curled into a smile. His gums and teeth were stained red from betel nut juice. "Wouldn't you like to guarantee yourself the best results possible?"

"Yes. Yes, I would like that very much."

"Then make a donation to Manasa, the mother of snakes. She will bless you."

৪১

Over their long period of coexistence, snakes and humans have shared a strange relationship. While our close-up vision may have evolved because they are the only threats that need to be seen from close quarters, our imagination has cast them in a whole spectrum of heroic and villainous roles.

Mythology instructs us to associate their limbless slithering bodies with deceit and lies. Their forked tongues are distrustful because the ends point in opposite directions. This is reiterated in literature, too, whether the book of Genesis or *Harry Potter and the Deathly Hallows*.

But humans are also taught to revere snakes. They are the figurative guardians of holy shrines, and across many cultures, their blood or still-beating hearts are consumed in the belief that the drinker will be blessed with virility or long life.

India is often considered the land of snakes and in Hinduism, one might argue, snake worship comes right after cow worship in popularity. Imagine the awe of the first Hindus when they saw a snake shed its old skin and emerge anew. Could there be a finer representation in nature of the Karmic belief in birth, death, and rebirth? The *Bhagavad Gita* states that just like human beings discard old clothing to don new, so does the soul discard one body for another. But can religion alone be held accountable for every mysterious unanswered question? What's the role of cultural accoutrement? How else does one explain the centuries' old practice of snake charmers playing the flute, to which hooded cobras "dance?" How powerful it must feel to know gods can be reduced to commodities, that they can be turned into accessories of entertainment at our will.

The goddess of snakes is Manasa, whose name means "intention" or "spiritual" in Sanskrit. While she bears all the standard motifs of Hindu iconography—the lotus flower, multiple arms, bejeweled body, rich sari, and in some cases, the third eye—she also has hooded snakes coiled at her feet and entwined around her arms.

The festival of Nag Panchami is dedicated to snakes. On that day, their icons and images are worshipped. Live snakes are offered milk and gifts, such as incense, flowers, and coconuts in the hope they will bless the worshipper with wealth, knowledge, and fame. Nag Panchami is held in Shraavana, the fifth month of the Hindu calendar. It is the month of monsoons. It is also the month of my birth.

৪০

I felt the color rising in my cheeks. Shame overpowered outrage. This uneducated man and his cronies were feeding me religious drivel. They were robbing me in broad daylight, and I, the graduate of a posh college with a degree and internship to my name, was foolishly obeying their dictates. Was I really this powerless? Where was my spine? I tried to swallow and couldn't. My mouth tasted bitter. I was filled with acute hatred for myself. In spite of my awareness and disgust, I heard myself say, "Yes, of course I will donate to Manasa. I want the mother of snakes to bless me."

From an ocher-colored cloth bag I hadn't noticed until then, the leader scooped out a dirty brass bowl and thrust it into my face. "We pour in milk here whenever Manasa's children are hungry and need to be fed. Go on, put in your money. Then touch the bowl to your head, and Manasa will bless you instantly."

I felt my ability to see had gone into overdrive. The snakes seemed restless. Agitated. I could make out every single, hexagon-shaped scale, the play of light and shadow on their undulating bodies as they slithered on their masters—rippling, rising, and falling—while they examined my presence and tasted the air around them. I noticed their flat triangular heads, the two little gashes for nostrils, and the timeless length of their bodies. The perfect circles of their eyes reminded me of dead fish, cold and unblinking. But theirs were ringed with fire. "Evil eyes," I called them, but in a silent whisper inaudible even to myself. I feared they could read my mind, strip it bare of every good thought, and replace it with something primordial that would not negotiate nor listen to reason.

The largest of the snakes rode on the neck of the leader. In some primitive way, it had probably understood that as long as it was with this particular human being, it had nothing to fear. So it reached out, intent on understanding me better. It stroked the air between us in wavy arrows and positioned its face right in front of mine. Our eyes locked—mine out of terror and the snake's out of curiosity, our mouths mere kissing distance away.

Can snakes distinguish between human expressions of terror, devotion, awe? What about love? Do they have good memories? If Bollywood is to be believed, then yes. They are portrayed as vengeful entities that can and do track down those who have been cruel to them. But what created this idea? Or was this, too, a byproduct of our faith in their immortality?

The most disconcerting element was that this entire spectacle was unfolding in front of the enormous crowd gathered at the Savitri Cinema bus stop. There were only a handful of women. But in that moment, they were united with the men in watching this show, which the snakes and snake charmers were putting up at my expense. Sure, the men and women scanned the horizon every now and then for their respective buses, but otherwise, they kept their attention glued to me. I implored them with my eyes. I cried out to them in my head, but in typical New Delhi-style, no one stepped forward to help. But I truly had no right to be angry. If our roles been reversed and I had been one of them, I would have done exactly the same.

Once adrenaline registers that there might be danger, the human body weighs its options: *flight or fight?* In case both options are absent, adrenaline signals a third, called *tonic immobility*, meaning, *playing dead.* The body enters an almost dreamlike state of existence. There is a sense of detachment from the individual's own body, as if it is being watched from a distance.

Tonic immobility is *imposed* on the human body at the time of any medical operation, and even with anesthesia, the Reptilian Brain might interpret the surgical invasion as a threat and try to choose between the flight/fight mechanism. Which is often why, while recovering from operations, patients experience shivering—it's the nervous system's method of releasing the "charge" built up during the period of enforced immobility.

℘

I was moving so slowly, the leader could barely contain his impatience. He snapped, "Come, come, Madam, let us not delay this any further. Make your donation quickly."

"Would you like to keep one of the snakes?" One of his cronies joked. He had a high-pitched feminine voice that got muffled by the trio bursting into laughter.

"Yes," the third one chimed in, "looks like they have found mutual love."

My mind and body had been overtaken by someone, who in spite of watching hundreds of documentaries, had forgotten that snakes like these were not venomous. Defanged, they were harmless, which is why these men were using them in the first place. The only damage these snakes could inflict was crawling over someone's body and making her uncomfortable.

I pulled out the single currency note I had in my purse. It was fifty rupees, roughly equivalent to a dollar, but enough in the New Delhi of the early 2000s to get me through a couple of bus rides.

The men were not amused.

"Come on, Madam, search your bag thoroughly. Surely, you must have more cash."

"I don't. I am a college student. I'm an intern, but I haven't been paid yet. I have only been working there for a week."

"Are you lying to us?" The leader snarled. He inched closer.

"No!" My eyes filled with tears.

"Are you sure?"

"Yes."

"In that case, I hope Manasa will be pleased with your contribution. I cannot guarantee anything. Put the money inside the brass pot. Yes. Don't worry, my snake is just too friendly. It knows you are doing this to appease its mother. Now lift the pot and touch it to your forehead. Do you feel Manasa's blessings seeping into you? Do you feel her power?"

"Yes," I mumbled, hating myself and my existence.

"Go now." The man waved his hand dismissively. He put away my fifty-rupee note inside his shirt pocket.

"But. . . how? How will I reach my office? I don't have any money! You took it."

This time he stepped so close I could smell his

fetid breath, the salty stench of his underarms, and the snake, which oddly had no smell. His words were wrapped in a thin film of concern, "Are you suggesting that I, that we, *forced* the money out of you? Did you not give it to Manasa out of your own accord?"

The snake's head was a few centimeters away from mine. I could feel its movements rippling the air around my hair.

I stammered, "I… yes, I did. I did. I will go."

The leader laughed raucously and his brothers joined in. Then they turned around and began to walk away, but I remained rooted to my spot, my skin hot, my face angry and ashamed. I was stuck in between home and office. I did not have a single rupee left on me. I could not take any transport, nor could I make a phone call. And worse, I had allowed three "holy" men to rob me using harmless snakes as weapons.

An auto rickshaw pulled up next to me. Or maybe I smelled its diesel fumes moments before I heard its sputtering engine. The driver was a young man about my age. He had a round face and curly hair. He pointed in the direction of the snake charmers. "That was rough," he said. "I saw what happened."

I stared at the ground. My feet hurt from the high-heeled shoes. I suddenly had the urge to slip them off. "Don't remind me about it," I said.

The driver shrugged. "Get in. Let's get your money back."

I looked at him, at his confident eyes, his no-nonsense demeanor. I heard my father's cautionary voice in my head. How could I trust a complete stranger? Especially after what had just happened. What was wrong with me? Why did I consider getting into an auto without any money to my name? What if this man drove off with me somewhere else? Who would come to my rescue?

"Yes, let's," I said, jumping into the auto rickshaw. It had nothing to do with getting back my money. But it had everything to do with being able to face myself again.

As the engine kicked back to life, the driver said, "I couldn't really tell if you were giving them the money out of choice or it was being forced out of you. I decided to check when you didn't move even after they walked away."

"I was just too scared." Admitting the truth didn't make things any better.

"Don't you know those snakes can't do anything?"

"Yes, I know. I know."

We caught up with the snake charmers just as they were about to enter a residential neighborhood. The driver swerved around and blocked their passage. Without stepping out, he snapped, "Return her money right now, or I am calling the police."

"Why?" The leader smirked, "She gave it to us willingly. We did not touch her. Here, I'll ask her in front of you. Maybe then you will believe me."

There was something about the way he spoke that the driver and I instinctively knew what was about to happen. They were going to throw their snakes on me. How dare I enlist help and come chasing after them.

The driver swiftly jumped out. He positioned his body like a shield in front of me. "Stay exactly where you are," he warned the men. "You have no business with her. Just return her money and go."

The men glared. I scanned the quiet neighborhood. Miraculously, the situation didn't worsen.

The leader fished out the fifty-rupee note from his pocket and handed it to the driver. Then he stepped back and watched in silence as we drove away.

ಃ

I don't know why those three men decided to obey the young, curly-haired man that morning. Where did all their aggression disappear? What prevented them from taking him on? Perhaps there was a shared history, an unsettled debt from the past. I didn't probe, and the driver didn't offer any explanation.

He dropped me off at work, where he only accepted what was due to him and refused a tip. I wonder if he felt sorry for how little money I had. Maybe my helplessness shamed him.

Over the next several days, my flight instinct dominated my behavior pattern. I stopped wearing high-heeled shoes. I dug out muted cotton shirts and trousers. I constantly looked over my shoulder, expecting to see those three men walk up to me, call me *Madam* and stupefy me with their ochre robes and yellow snakes. The Savitri Cinema bus stop took on a ghoulish avatar in my imagination, and for several nights, I slept poorly.

I have seen such "holy men" operate in other parts of India as well. Their modus operandi is the same. They sell fear. I know their snakes cannot harm me, and yet I have taken ridiculous steps to avoid contact. I have taken preposterously longer routes, refused to get out of cars, and pasted myself to known and unknown people alike in order to disappear into the crowd. I know my Reptilian Brain registers the men—not just those who handle the reptiles, but also those who stand and watch, titillated by the possibilities of a lone woman circled by men and snakes.

On Collecting Stories

It was the first day of class, and I was already ten minutes late. *Great*, I thought, glancing at my watch. This was not the impressive start I was hoping for in my new life as a graduate student of creative writing at the University of Idaho. I hurtled toward the classroom. What if I were my American professor's first student from India? What if my tardiness would lead her to have a poor opinion of every Indian? But I couldn't help getting lost on this campus. The buildings all looked the same, like they did when I researched American universities back in India, like they do in brochures and university websites—tall, red-brick edifices surrounded by flowerbeds and expansive trees, and every few steps, solemn stone benches dedicated to so-and-so, where students lounge wearing headphones, their armor against the world and anyone who might want to approach for help.

Only three days ago, I had arrived in Moscow, Idaho. In many ways, it still hadn't sunk in that I was actually in America. I had nurtured this dream since I was nine years old and read *The Adventures of Huckleberry Finn*. Huck, with his fierce temperament and taste for adventure, had seemed the most badass boy in the world. I had fallen in love with his integrity and loyalty, qualities I felt he strove to hide under layers of irreverence.

That same year, we learned about America in my social studies class in school. Our textbook had a chapter titled, *Superpowers of the World*, because back in 1989, there did exist two superpowers. There were beautiful photographs highlighting the natural wonders of America and the Soviet Union, but the one that gripped me was of a Los Angeles freeway system, a bird's eye view of a complex web of roads, a mesh of threads tautly strung by a giant's enormous hands. I was blown away by the idea that there could be so many journeys to embark upon. I remember staring at the photograph for hours, wondering who drove on those roads, how they even knew which one to pursue. I wanted to be a passenger with them and have for myself the same adventure.

Eighteen years later, here I was in America, my port of entry, Los Angeles. It was an emotional moment when my feet touched the ground at LAX. I walked down a narrow carpeted aisle, my jumbled thoughts clashed with the loud broadcasts over the public announcement system. I neither wanted to jump nor scream nor call my parents in New Delhi to assure them I had landed safely. No, I wanted to stand quietly in a corner and savor the moment—of the many languages I overheard, the acrid smell of perfumes mingling with sweat and detergent, the busyness of the customs and immigration officers—and congratulate myself for having accomplished the dream I had nurtured all these years.

I boarded a smaller plane to reach Idaho. I had studied my new hometown, Moscow, through the city's website and through Google images. Still, it was a surprise. It wasn't just starkly different from the organized chaos I had known all my life in New Delhi, but also from the slight taste I got of LA. Moscow was compact and peaceful. Its homes were large and spacious with trimmed lawns and gardens growing neat rows of herbs, zucchini, and tomatoes. It was the end of summer, but people were still out barbequing and shopping at the local farmers' market. Everywhere I looked, there seemed to be an air of prosperity and conviviality, far removed from the miseries of daily life I had grown accustomed to in India. Strangers charmingly held doors open for everyone, including me, and enquired, "How's it going?" The sidewalks looked like they were shampooed every morning. I couldn't see a spot of dirt anywhere. Nor pollution. No homelessness, no beggars, no visible poverty. It was antiseptic and unreal, a city carved out of a movie set, and its residents were actors born to enact their roles. Happy and carefree, they drank their drip coffees and biked everywhere, and an invisible shield cocooned them from wars, drones, and starvation elsewhere.

By the time I located the classroom and walked in, I was twenty minutes late. Fifteen students and a professor sat in a circle around two large tables joined together. A few smiled as I entered the room. I was the only nonwhite person. I wasn't intimidated or scared. It wasn't as if I hadn't interacted with white people before. But those interactions had been in India, limited to conversations with exchange students and international colleagues or a handful of my father's foreign friends.

But I did feel like an Outsider, the same way I had on my first day of college at St. Stephen's in Delhi. I had looked at my male classmates and walked out of the room, convinced I had made a mistake. For twelve years leading up to that day, I had studied at a Catholic, girls-only school.

At the professor's request, my classmates began introducing themselves. They listed their names, prior education, hometowns, etc. In India, I had always prided myself in being aware of my surroundings, in my ability to distinguish between accents from various parts of the country, or in terms of picturing someone's hometown, irrespective of how far it was from New Delhi. But here I struggled as I tried locating my classmates' hometowns in my mind: Where was Missoula? Was Nebraska a city or a state? Did Oregon have a coastline?

I excused my ignorance, and in my mind, I smudged the locations into one big glob. It was all America, wasn't it? How different could it be? I dismissed the lengths and experiences of my classmates' "local" travel. Surely, since I had covered the longest geographical distance to be here, *I* had the most important story to tell. Since I was the *person of color* from a *third-world country*, *I* had the most at stake.

All those years ago, my first exposure to America had been through Huck Finn, who had most definitely known his fair share of hardship and poverty, but three days in Moscow had erased stories like his from my mind. I did not see real flesh and blood people around me. I chose to see caricatures straight out of a Hollywood film— their body language, nationality, and the color of their skin granting them the kind of privilege the rest of the world often associates with Americans.

Like me, most of my classmates were in their twenties. Healthy and fresh, they were still aglow from summer's tan. I imagined their lives echoing predictable storylines, where no matter what happens in the beginning and the middle, things always straighten out by the end.

I awarded myself a smug smile: What could these squeaky clean people know of the human condition, of actual adversity? What could they possibly teach me about the meaning of life or the curiosity and gratification inherent in it? As if any one of them had ever gone hungry. Not that I had, but poverty and hunger are inescapable realities in India. Part your curtain or crack open a window, and there they are—curled next to each other on the footpath, dressed in rags and cowering from the police under the bridge, defiantly looking you in the eye.

I felt deliciously burdened by my worldliness and epic travel, by my romantic story in terms of how I came to be in America. I already owned a master narrative. It wasn't really mine, but it had been bequeathed to me thanks to my family's messy history. I had heard it since I was a child—how in 1947, when India won freedom after two hundred years of British rule, the country was cleaved into two, killing millions and displacing many more. Both sides of my grandparents were evicted from their ancestral villages in what is now Bangladesh, and overnight, they became refugees. The move cost them friends and family, and it took them years to rebuild their lives and build new homes. Back in India, I had accepted these stories with a sense of awe, but here I felt burdened by them in a good, writerly sort of a way. How could any one of my classmates ever match the depth of my history and narrative?

I can't pinpoint the exact moment my classmates stopped being Americans in my eyes and became people instead, just as ordinary, flawed, complex, and brilliant as those I had left behind. I was swept away by what we read in class—books by authors like Nick Flynn and Kathryn Harrison—that shattered my long-held assumptions about boundaries one must never cross in writing and storytelling. But it was my classmates' essays that broke my back and brought me to my knees. Their stories and essays dealt with wide-ranging themes, such as urban poverty and violence, alcoholism and drug addiction, forest fires and logging accidents, dysfunctional families and intergenerational conflict.

Once upon a time, it had been easy for me to dismiss complex tales in fiction as mere figments of their authors' imagination. But this was different. I knew these people. They weren't characters inside books I could read, enjoy, and put away on the shelf. They were my classmates. Friends. I was embarrassed by my earlier naiveté because the simple, yet shocking, truth was that some of my classmates—the same blonde, beautiful, and white Americans whose lives I had once deemed perfect—had lead hard painful lives and overcome unbelievable obstacles.

Case in point: one evening, a classmate read aloud an essay about his absentee alcoholic father. I couldn't stop myself and blurted out, "That is insane. Fathers are supposed to take care of their children." I realized how stupid I sounded the moment the words left my mouth, more so when a friend leaned in and whispered, "Yes, but not everyone does." It shook me to my core.

But even greater epiphanies were in store for me, and they entered my life once I started teaching writing. We read writers such as Cheryl Strayed and Marie Nasta, and emboldened by their words, my students wrote their own truths. I struggled to match their tidy appearances with the messiness of their lives as they unfolded on paper—stories of the young man coaxed into drugs by his best friend's father, the woman raped by her neighbor, the sister who saw her brother die before her eyes, and the grandfather torn between faith and temptation.

These stories drummed into my head something that I didn't want to admit: it was I who had lived a life of privilege. Born in a middle-class family with an engineer father and a stay-at-home mother, I was sent to good schools and raised to believe in myself. I was given the freedom to study anything I wanted, and imparted the confidence that if I truly put my mind to something, one day, it would be mine. And here I was, reading essays from students, some of whom couldn't even remember the last time they had heard an encouraging word from an adult.

I have now spent almost a decade in Moscow's tidy compactness. I teach on this same campus where once I was a student. I know this landscape so well I am rarely late to anything. Some days, I loudly complain about the grading load and indifferent students, and yet, every semester I approach their essays with equal parts excitement and trepidation. A few years ago, I visited Bangladesh and was privileged to witness my family's story up close. I haven't forgotten who I am, but I have also learned to carry my students' stories, the same way I once carried Huck's.

The Snow-White Men of India

The New Delhi I left behind in 2006 to study creative writing in Idaho was one I understood. We did not always see eye to eye, especially when it came to how often the city looked the other way with regards to making its women feel safe. Or its lack of reliable public transit options. Or the challenges of maintaining friendships in that busy metropolis of fifteen million people.

Still, it was a New Delhi that was comfortable in the way comfort is inherent in all hometowns. I was conversant with its roads. I had memorized the bus routes. I knew which neighborhoods to avoid after dark and which hole-in-the-wall establishments to frequent for the best sheermal and lamb brain masala. My strongest pop-culture memories of that time comprise the handful of malls where my friends and I used to hang out or watch movies, the almost non-existent presence of reality shows on Indian television, and the availability of only one brand of skin fairness cream—its distinct lavender-colored tube available for purchase at every corner shop.

In 2011, however, when I revisited India after a gap of three years, New Delhi was unrecognizable. As we drove from the international airport toward my parents' home, I heard about the new and excellent public transit system, which had not only shrunk vast distances but also made the city a lot safer. There were shiny roads snaking around dazzling new buildings, and more malls than I could count, thanks in part to the recently held Commonwealth Games. Although these glass and chrome constructions took away some of New Delhi's historic magnificence, I still felt a surge of pride. Now, a first-time traveler's initial impression of my hometown could only be favorable.

For the first few weeks, I lost myself in my mother's cooking, while my eyes and ears greedily wolfed down hours of non-English TV programs. I vegetated on the same red leather beanbag I had purchased with my first real salary nearly ten years ago and reread all my favorite books from childhood. I visited old friends and members of my extended family, and slowly, very slowly, I began to notice other changes brought on by India's rising economic presence in the world along with the enormous purchasing power of its new middle class. Normal regular people I had gone to school with were now posting giddy updates on Facebook about impulsive shopping trips, where they had parted with 60,000 rupees (approximately $1000) in less than ten minutes. The country now seemed rife with an alarming number of do-gooders, mostly with political backgrounds, each of them armed with an array of causes both pseudo and genuine, and the number of reality TV shows was proportionate to the number of Indians in the world.

But what surprised me the most was how skin care had become synonymous with fairness creams. While most of these were, expectedly, targeted toward women—both the young and the not-so-young—there were also a handful promising salvation to men. The tubs, tubes, and pots were everywhere—on giant hoardings flanking busy streets, inside expensive makeup and skin-care salons, in full-length newspaper and magazine inserts, and of course, on TV screens. They were modeled by celebrities as well as by regular-next-door-neighbor-type folks. The visuals were remarkably similar, their pitch written as if by the same team of copywriters: you dabbed on the fairness cream, and within days, you blossomed into a better whiter version of yourself. Because whiteness imparts confidence. Because whiteness emboldens you to look straight into the camera or into the eyes of other people, whom you may have hitherto avoided. Because whiteness automatically firms your posture and lengthens your legs so you can stride to interviews with aplomb, and from there, land your dream job, become a rock star, and get the date you have been eyeing since forever.

Intrigued, I searched online for "how to whiten your skin naturally." I was bombarded with websites ranging from helpful to hysterical. The list of suggested ingredients included saffron and sandalwood pastes; milk from cows, almonds, and coconut; tomato pulp and papaya pulp; potato slices and cucumber slices; pressed hibiscus flower; rose water; ground-up oats; lavender oil and tea tree oil; radish juice and lemon juice. Basically, everything short of the tears of a unicorn diluted with the blood of a virgin.

It couldn't have been more ironic given the daily realities I confront in my current hometown of Moscow, Idaho—possibly one of the whitest towns in America. For the most part, since my arrival, Moscow has been accepting of my foreign nonwhite existence, although there have been a few instances where my color has seemingly suggested that I must not understand English very well, so questions have been shouted at me. Not knowing a particular language is the same as being hard of hearing. At other times, my brownness has prompted well-meaning folks to stop me on sidewalks, intercept me at cafes, or slide next to me at bus stops and ask, with beatific smiles and concerned expressions, if I have heard the name of their Lord, Jesus Christ. I have politely assured them that I have and that he was a most wonderful man, and they have wisely dropped the issue there.

But each year, especially after spring and summer vacations, Moscow's obsession with Brownness really comes to shine, as numerous students can be overheard enviously comparing each other's tans. They gush over new and trendy tanning products; they pick and defend their favorites; and they carefully sort through incentives, such as the one offered at the gym I frequent, where tanning services are included for members at no extra cost. Sometimes there are accidents—when perfectly normal white students return to school orange, and it takes them the remainder of the semester to reacquire the color they were born with. All this, of course, is only an echo of what often gets peddled as the ideal form of beauty on American television and in cinema, where a certain kind of brown equals sunshine, athleticism, youth, and beauty.

The exact opposite of the message conveyed in India.

A similar search of homemade tanning products throws up its own cornucopia of ingredients. These include henna paste, organic black tea, vanilla extract, ground cinnamon and nutmeg, raw cocoa, oils leached from rosemary and coconut, coffee grounds, brown sugar, crushed almonds, aloe vera gel, and carrots.

The stark contrast between India and America reminds me of an incident from my own college days. The year was 1997. India was celebrating its fiftieth anniversary of independence, which is probably why *Border*, a jingoistic Hindi film bashing on Pakistan became the country's biggest commercial blockbuster. It marked Bill Clinton's election to his second term in office, and J. K. Rowling delivered the very first *Harry Potter*.

For me, it was an important year because I was accepted into St. Stephen's College, one of India's finest colleges and best-known repository of the Oxbridge (Oxford-Cambridge) culture it has acquired as an indirect result of colonization. Given the nationally-ranked status of St. Stephen's and its hallowed history (Gandhi had been a regular visitor), my classmates and I were convinced, at age eighteen, that life from this point onward was going to be an endless Ferris wheel ride of one successful venture after another. After all, we were in the most meritocratic institution ever imaginable; we had fought hard and studied harder to get here.

But one afternoon, I was rudely reminded of the real world, layered with faults and discriminations awaiting us outside the majestic gates of St. Stephen's upon graduation. I was with a friend, Sita, a girl the same age as me and the exact shade of brown. We were drinking lemonade at the Café (a singular St. Stephen's institution) when Sita asked, "Do you feel self-conscious about your dark skin?"

I was stunned, not because up to that point, I had been unaware of my own skin tone or that many Indians prefer light-skinned children and partners, but because I had naïvely assumed that once you became a Stephanian, no one challenged your place in the world over something as trivial as the color of your skin. I kept quiet, unsure how to answer.

Oblivious of my state, Sita continued, "My parents will start looking for a suitable bridegroom as soon as I graduate."

"What do you mean 'suitable'?"

"Just the usual. A boy from Kerala, same church, denomination, language, etc."

This time I didn't hide my outrage. "What is the point of studying at Stephen's if you are going to let your parents choose your groom, and worse, he has to be the exact checklist of *their* virtues?"

Sita was silent for a minute. Then she shrugged. "I agree with you. But I also know I will obey them. I don't want to be the cause of any tension, although my mother has already said that finding me a groom will be difficult given my color. At her insistence, I have begun applying a lemon juice and turmeric face pack every morning."

I no longer remember the rest of our conversation. Maybe we argued over the relationship between people's suitability vis-à-vis their skin color. Or maybe we switched over to another topic. But the incident made me aware, for the first time in my life, that even though I might not be directly perpetuating prejudices, they will always find a way to integrate with my subconscious and with my larger world.

These days, Sita and I are friends on Facebook, where in the manner of most virtual friendships, we never speak to each other. I see pictures of her husband, who is several shades darker than her. And yet, I can venture this with certainty—at the time of their wedding, no questions must have been raised about his suitability (or lack thereof) based on his color, but hers might have escalated discussions to the level of a grave national disaster.

And it's also not just Sita. I have at least two other friends—one an editor in a leading publishing house and the other a biologist—who belong to two different religions and regions of India, speak different mother tongues, and are both academically more qualified than their husbands, and yet, they, too, have endured the same hurtful jabs about their complexions from their parents or in-laws.

It is no secret that like in many other parts of Asia and Africa, in India, too, fair skin equals attractiveness. It denotes power and superiority, which are problematic notions given India's class-based, caste-based history as well as colonization. Being fair-skinned is associated with the upper class, whether Brahmins or Englishmen, who could hold on to the milky-whiteness of their skin as opposed to everyone else who did backbreaking work outside. The mindset is so damaging and deep-rooted that pick up any matrimonial ad, whether in the print media or online, and the demand for a "fair" wife is as timeless and relentless as the Indian sun.

But the last time I was in India, I derived a small frisson of pleasure from the fact that fairness creams, moisturizers, sunscreens, and lotions were no longer solely targeted toward women. Sure, the first fairness cream for men was launched in India in 2005, twenty-seven years *after* they were for women. But still, I was happy to note that even the most accomplished brown man could no longer afford to be complacent. Instead, he now faced the same pressure to snow-whiten himself as his female counterpart, whether his objective was to become more suitable for the marriage market, for the professional world, or his overall individual growth. And just for this—a barely leveled playing field—I allowed myself a smug bittersweet victory, comparable to how I feel every time I witness the search for that perfect shade of brown in my little white corner of America.

On Seeking Answers

I was hungry that evening, but the questions I asked my brother had nothing to do with food. It felt strange to be famished in an environment where food had served as an anchor, our one constant reality. My brother must have been hungry, too, perhaps more than I was, but he buried it under his characteristic calmness. I asked him, "Where are so many tears coming from? How is it that they are not stopping? Do you know?" He shook his fourteen-year-old head at me, his twenty-two-year-old sister, and reached out to hold my hand.

We were lying side-by-side in one of the bedrooms of the house in which Dida, our maternal grandmother, had died only a day before. Primary and secondary sounds reached us every now and then from the world that lay outside the bedroom's walls. A concerned voice offered to cook something and feed the children in the house, a tired-with-all-the-surrounding-despair voice began making lists of things to buy for the worship ceremonies starting the next day, and a third voice, obviously ignorant of Hindu cremation rites, asked if all the men of the family would have to shave their heads. I tightened my grip around my brother's fingers. Our entwined hands were clammy though it was only March. The ceiling was black but switching on the lights wouldn't have made a difference.

My brother and I and our parents had flown in to Calcutta from New Delhi that very morning. Sundry relatives had picked us up from the airport and driven us to the death house. There, Dida's already-cold body was being frozen and preserved before it could be offered to holy Hindu flames and reduced to ashes. In that one smoky process, where our primordial fire-worshipping souls were going to come together and function as a community, we were going to burn all tangible evidence of a life that had existed:

Once breathed.

Laughed loudly.

Made inappropriate jokes, at all times, and at everyone's expense. Even in front of the children. I owe my stock of Bengali slangs to her.

Knitted the most disproportionate clothes for my dolls from scraps left over from bigger, more important stitching and sewing projects. All the clothes, thus, had mismatched sleeves.

Told the most unimaginative yet completely original fairytales. There was once a story about an old man, his confused wife, and the ghost that lived in their attic. It was awful. The story made no sense, more so because Dida fell asleep in the middle of telling it, and her loud snores prevented me from finding what the ghost did to the old man and his wife.

Insisted on telling the whole neighborhood about her granddaughter's real and imagined achievements.

Possessed able, slightly dry, yellow-stained hands from a lifetime of turmeric usage. I never saw her square-shaped nails not stained yellow. When I was a kid, Dida and I used to play a game, where I would grab her hands playfully, study her palms, rub her nails, wrinkle my nose, and say, "Dida, you have dirty hands!" And she would flash back, "Fine, you make your own fish curry from now." I would launch into a long stream of protests, and we would both collapse into heaps of laughter.

Dida's was a life that adhered to its own, sometimes bizarre, composition of colors and conditions, and she could have single-handedly organized an art exhibition and called it, *My Way or the Highway.* In spite of finding faults with the exhibit, I would have attended. Fierce, feisty, unputdownable women are magic, after all. And those, like my Dida, are impossible to come across twice.

ॐ

My grandmother was born on April 8, 1928, in Dhaka, present-day Bangladesh. The daughter of a physician and the youngest of eight siblings, she was married off as soon as a "good boy" was found for her. She was fifteen, he was thirty, but good he certainly was. His name was Amulya. He had been unmarried all this while because as the eldest son of his traditional family, it had been his duty to marry off all his younger sisters and educate or find employment for his brothers. Only after that could he be so selfish to think of himself and the hopes and dreams he had for his own life. In 1947, British India got partitioned into two—India and Pakistan—and that's when they moved to Calcutta for good. By then, they already had a son. In Calcutta, they had two more—a daughter (my mother), followed by a son. That's where

Dida lived the rest of her life and died in 2002.

The story of my life with Dida began in 1979, and I have yet to find all the ways in which it continues to live on.

⅋

For the longest time that evening, my brother and I lay side-by-side, and no one came to interrupt our silence. The sounds from outside continued to reach us every now and then. Someone made tea for the third, fourth, fifth time. A tap gurgled. A spoon fell and clattered on the mosaic floor. *Why are Bengalis obsessed with tea? Why do we drink it by the buckets?* I wondered. But my mind vaporized those questions. Instead, I asked my brother, "If it hurts so much now, how much will it hurt when it's Ma or Baba? Or one of us?" Again, he didn't answer. He kept his hold on my hand. Dida's youngest grandchild comforted her oldest with his stoic solid presence. "Do all fourteen-year-old boys know how to deal with grief?" I asked him silently, "Do they all know when to listen to questions quietly and not offer any answers because I am not really seeking them?"

⅋

When my brother and I were younger, summer vacations meant going to Calcutta to visit everyone in the "hometown." Our parents assiduously drummed it into our heads that New Delhi, our current place of residence, was only a temporary home. Calcutta was permanent. It had been their hometown and so it was ours as well. When we were kids, we didn't protest, because neither of us understood the fine differences between the two cities.

We probably loved the idea because Calcutta equaled grandparents, aunts and uncles, new books, indulgence and affection, monsoons, mangoes, coconut and sugarcane juice, and weekend trips to the coast, with its accompanying boat rides and fried fish. So every year, when schools closed mid-May, Ma would bundle her two children and leave New Delhi, only to return sometime in the first week of July, just a few days before the schools reopened. Sometimes, our father would accompany us but only for a short period because offices, of course, don't feel the need for two-month vacations. So he stayed on in New Delhi, while the three of us embraced Calcutta and its peculiarities.

My earliest and fondest memories of Dida are from about this time and nearly all of them revolve around food. Even before we showed up at her apartment, Dida would stock up the fridge with temptations ranging from mangos to fish curries in mustard paste to everything in between. There was *pataligurer payesh*, a rice pudding cooked with basmati rice, whole milk, and jaggery, the coarse brown sugar made from the sap of palm trees. Dida fragranced it with bay leaves and garnished it with raisins, and in my eyes, it shone like gold. There was also *malpoa*—rich, dark-brown dumplings soaked in sugar syrup—and *patishapta*, rice flour crepes stuffed with sweet coconut filling. I can still taste Dida's fish curries. They were light because they had minimal oil; they were yellow because their main spice was turmeric; and they were sprinkled with black dots because of the nigella seeds that swam in the gravy. But her grandest concoction was something she called *titar dal*, or "bitter lentils." It was far from bitter though. Soup-like in consistency, *titar dal*'s main ingredients were yellow lentils, vegetables such as bitter gourd and green gourd, and the seasonings included ginger paste, clarified butter, mustard seeds, green chilies, salt, and a pinch of sugar. Dida insisted it was the best thing to eat in a hot country. The "cool" vegetables and minimal spices kept the body free from toxins. I couldn't have cared. It tasted great like everything else at her home, and that's all that mattered.

Food also provided the background for showcasing Dida's remarkably loud and often inappropriate sense of humor. She belonged to the generation where demureness was expected of a woman. But that wasn't her. She loved passionately, loyally, and ferociously. She had a laugh that started in her belly and ricocheted like fireworks. If you got caught in it, it swept you off like a tsunami. But if you were wrong, no matter how much she loved you, she would set you straight. Affection, kindness, and generosity of spirit were not going to come in the way.

One time when she was visiting us in New Delhi, I happened to make fun of the senility that was going to set in any day now owing to her age. She laughed along, enjoying the joke, but unbeknownst to me, also made up her mind about teaching me a lesson.

That very evening, Dida set about making *patishapta*. The initial batch was wonderful as expected. Light and sweet, the crepes were like little gifts. When she made the second batch, she set aside one from it. "Eat it, Didun," she said, calling me the affectionate name she had always used for me. She ladled it onto my plate. "This one is especially for you."

I opened my mouth wide and greedily took a bite. The crepe was flat. It tasted of nothing except plain dough. I raised my eyebrows and looked at her quizzically.

"Are you sure? I am not tasting anything."

"Of course there is. Take a bigger bite. I have crammed this one with raisins."

I took another bite and then another. Nothing. There was not a drop of sweetness anywhere. I couldn't find one raisin nor a shred of coconut. I looked at her again, puzzled.

This time she started laughing. "Now who is senile, huh?" she asked.

Food defined Dida's relationships, and right up to her last days, Dida believed that people who enjoy food in all its aspects—cooking, eating, and feeding others— are warm and large-hearted. In other words, a person's worth and humanity are directly proportionate to the well-stockedness of her fridge, larder, kitchen counter, etc. I always knew my mother had inherited this peculiar belief system. Today, as I maintain an independent life and kitchen of my own, I know I do, too.

ॐ

Over the period of time, as one summer vacation merged into another, my brother and I grew up. Grandparents and indulgence stopped being enough. Life needed to be faster, quicker, smarter. Calcutta seemed decaying, dying, and in fact, almost dead. New Delhi was comfortable, and summer vacations could be spent here with friends. Or we could go somewhere completely new. India was a big country, after all. Where was the need to go to Calcutta every year? Why did *we* have to go every time? Why couldn't *they* come here instead? And so we began to protest: Calcutta was boring. It had fewer entertainment options as compared to New Delhi. All we did there was eat and visit relatives. Calcutta was hot, wet, and sweaty. My brother gave it an alternate name, "Ghaam-land," or the "Land of Sweat." And he and I both began to take offence every time our parents told others that our stay in New Delhi was temporary and that some day, we were all going to return to Calcutta. *No*, we protested, *this was our home*.

I think Dida was one person who instinctively felt the change. I wonder what gave it away. A disinterested voice on the telephone? Our lackluster enthusiasm despite her dining table and fridge shelves groaning from the weight of all the food? Or a delayed response to her letters? Whatever it was, I know she understood and tried to fit in.

She began writing her letters to me in English. While previously she had always written in Bengali, I think Dida decided it was time for a switch when she guessed that Bengali had started to lose its appeal in favor of English. Her standard postcards now arrived with a difference. The handwriting was still just as untidy, but now it was shakier. Somehow unsure.

I, the desperate-to-be-cool teenager, did not see the effort that had gone into writing the postcard. I did not understand the despair of an old woman, frustrated by the growing distance between her and her oldest grandchild and worried that the paternal grandparents—with their exemplary writing skills in English—might score higher points. All I remember is laughing unkindly at the effort.

Another time, I decided to check her general knowledge. So I quizzed her, "You watch the news AND read the newspaper every day, don't you, Dida?"

"Yes," she said, scrunching her eyes, unsure of

where the conversation was headed.

"Will you please answer a quick question?"

"Sure."

"Who is the president of America?"

"Isn't it Kennedy?"

The year was 1998. It was Bill Clinton's second term, and Dida was visiting us from Calcutta. She was our guest. She, who had fed us feasts and treated us like royalty every time we were in her home. But after hearing her answer, I marched off to find my mother. "Why couldn't your mother just say, 'I don't know?' Why did she have to lie, Ma? How could she not know something this simple? She sits in front of the TV every evening. This, I tell you, is downright embarrassing!"

Today when I remember that episode, I want to go back in time and slap my fourteen-year-old self. I see the futility of that misplaced indignation. Why did Dida *have* to know the details of a president whose presence or absence did not touch her existence in any which way? When John F. Kennedy took his oath on January 20, 1961, Dida was thirty-three years old. I wonder if some part of her responded to Kennedy's charm, good looks, or to something else equally transient she saw on TV or on the pages of the newspaper. It captured a photograph of the frozen-in-time, forever-young Kennedy and embedded itself in her mind.

ॐ

Calcutta's cremation grounds smell of death, chaos, rituals, and long lines of sweaty Hindus. They lack the sophistication that Hindu philosophy centers around: that Atman or our Individual Soul is never really ours. It is part of the Brahman or the Universal Soul. Atman never dies; it is only the body that does. Atman is a permanent participant in the crazy, Ferris wheel circle of birth, death, and rebirth based on the cumulative karma the person has gathered in this life. The Ferris wheel goes on and on until the time Atman reaches a stage of perfection. At that point, it attains Moksha. Emancipation. Escape.

As soon as we reached the cremation grounds that afternoon, some of my family members set about negotiating the price of rites and all the necessary articles. I overheard identical conversations and negotiations going on in lines parallel to our own. In an overcrowded country, death is not a private affair. The air was thick and obtuse with sacred Sanskrit chants, fresh and wilted flowers, the aroma of incense sticks—sandalwood, rose, jasmine—the heat of Calcutta in March, smug bargains and deals, and the salty smell of old age, sweat, and tears.

I let my mind wander. I did not want my grandmother's soul to be judged by some abstract reality up above and beyond my realm of understanding. I wanted something more tangible. If it were left to me, I would have sanctioned an alien abduction of her soul rather than this karma judgment politburo. Surely, not all alien encounters have to do with medical testing or sexual procedures. I remember at least one *X-Files* episode where the abductee returns looking quite refreshed and pleased with herself. The judgment of karma sounds harsh, cruel, unkind, and enormously subjective. Alien abduction, on the other hand, has a ring of excitement, adventure, perhaps even coolness to it. It seems something Dida would choose herself. If John Edward Mack, a professor at Harvard Medical School, could publicly investigate and publish his findings after a study of over 200 test cases of men and women who claimed to have been abducted by aliens, then why couldn't I hold on to this theory? If some of Mack's subjects could insist that they came back with heightened spiritual awareness and concern for the environment, then why was it wrong for me to imagine that at this very moment in time, Dida's soul, too, was alternating between two dichotomous truths?

The first truth wanted her to get inside a body, either the old wrinkled one that she had worn until two days ago, or a new tight thing that she might have picked up a few moments ago from the wardrobe section of the spacecraft. Next, she would need appropriate clothing. What colors would she choose? I know she liked all shades of red, the color that Hinduism recognizes as representative of marriage, and therefore, not permitted to widows. Dida's husband, my grandfather, died a year before my birth, so I never saw her wear anything remotely close to red. She spent her life with whites, creams, and pastels, and occasional browns, blues, and purples, but I know her heart lay in red because she encouraged and indulged my own love for that color.

Dida's new body, now draped in red, might ask her to let go of all the benefits afterlife was dangling in front of her—eternal youth, freedom from pain and sickness, constant mobility—conditions that she hadn't been able to enjoy in her last few years on earth, just so she could be with her grandchildren one more time. Just for the joy of hearing their laughter, of watching them eat a meal in whose preparation she might have hovered over the flames for hours.

But the second version of this reality could be

Dida moving on and enjoying the benefits of her brand new adventure, most of which would still revolve around food and laughter. It could be that right this minute, Dida is with her new friends. Tall aliens with skinny frames. Giant heads with waxy cheeks. Sunken but sparkly eyes gleaming against tiny rosebud mouths. Would they be sheathed in any clothing? Maybe robes in opulent blues, blacks, silvers, and indigos—all colors of the universe. Maybe they have circled Dida, and she is holding court on a multitude of topics. One minute she is recounting a joke or a favorite memory or describing a grandchild's cherished toy. The spacecraft is thrumming with her loud boisterous laughter. The aliens have joined in, either out of respect for their formidable guest or because they are too intimidated to say "No." They are captivated by her quick efficiency. Scared into submission by her no-nonsense dictatorship. But any moment now they will discover the generosity of her spirit and see through her charade of aggression, especially once she makes them a perfect pot of chai—with the best quality tea leaves and the exact amount of milk, sugar, and brewing. Then they will learn how to hold teacups in their two-digit hands. Also, how to nibble on biscuits and acquire a taste for them. Not too many at a time. Just one for every cup.

Once done with tea—the good Bengali staple—Dida will instruct them to land at the Gangetic Delta. There, they will catch some hilsa because, as everyone knows, life without good fish is simply unfortunate and not worth living. Even if it is extraterrestrial.

She will send off the alien who looks like he can be bullied the most easily. Meekly, he will gather his robes and get her the fish she needs. He will assist her in the spaceship's kitchen, where he will spend the next few hours mastering the finest aspects of Bengali culinary sciences: how to distinguish between good and perfect turmeric, the right amount of salt needed for frying hilsa, and why mustard oil brings out the best flavor of this particular union of spices.

Throughout this entire exercise, Dida will make loud, dirty, inappropriate jokes, usually at the aliens' expense and right in front of them. Some would be filled with choicest Bengali slangs. Others would be plain bawdy. She will thus safeguard her reputation of being politically incorrect. Or should the term now be "astronomically incorrect?"

છ૦

I come back to the only reality I know. This black room, the double bed, the cotton bedspread, and my brother's fingers entwined around mine. Our hands have taken on a unity of their own. It's as if one doesn't want to let go of the other; they have dealt with enough loss for one day. I toy with the idea of telling my brother what I am thinking. Aliens, spacecrafts, chais, hilsas. . . what will he think? What will he say? Worse, what if in the midst of my monologue, one of our myriad family members walks in and overhears our conversation? The house is right now stacked and shelved with relatives and cousins. For my wonderful theories, will they not think of me as delusional? Will they not try and explain to me that the theory of alien abduction has no credibility?

But then, how will they tackle my counter claim, "Fine. There are no aliens. Let's discuss Karma, Nirvana, Moksha, shall we? Lend them your hundred-percent credibility. Make me believe that these things exist. That you know for sure this is exactly what we'll all go through. Can you do that?"

My mind goes back to the other reality I saw today. The fire that consumed my grandmother's once beautiful hands, her steel and silver hair, the tired body where unpronounceable diseases built permanent homes, and the feet that stopped supporting the rest of her. It was the same fire that Hindus consider Divine. The one we have worshipped since 1500 B.C.E. in the belief that it is a piece of the Sun God, that its upward shooting flames can take the devotee's prayers straight to the heavens, and that its heat and light have the power to dispel ignorance, darkness, and evil.

But today, the holy flames did none of that. They did not make any allowance for Dida, in spite of all her cooking, large-heartedness, spunky humor, and all the negotiations that my brother and I would have gladly and persistently done with the powers-that-be on her behalf. Instead, the flames just devoured. Perhaps, they, too, were hungry.

Goddesses

Although I never met her, I am told my great-grandmother, Basantamayi, was a deeply religious woman. She and her husband, my great-grandfather Bipin Chandra, lived in village Fatehabad, district Chittagong, in present day Bangladesh. He worked in the Excise Department for the British Government, and his life revolved around books and erudition, while Basantamayi moored hers to the various gods and goddesses of the Hindu pantheon. She could recite lengthy verses from the epics *Ramayana* and *Mahabharata* purely from memory. She followed scriptural dictates of purity and pollution incumbent on high-caste Hindus faithfully and performed domestic duties to perfection.

Basantamayi means *Forever Spring*, faintly ironic, considering she was married off at age ten to Bipin Chandra. He was twice her age. While to modern audiences this number might be preposterous, in her world, it was already a year too late. Among high-caste Hindu families of Bengal at that time, the prescribed age for marriage for girls was nine. Unfortunately, Basantamayi's parents were so dirt poor they had to wait a year to put together the minimum trousseau for their daughter.

Bipin Chandra and his parents were somewhat different from the norm. Not only did they not demand a dowry, they were also not perturbed by her "advanced" age. But other members of the extended family were not so kind. And so on her first day in her new home, ten-year-old Basantamayi, nervous bride, shy daughter-in-law, overheard complaints from a myriad of aunts, uncles, and neighbors: "Why this old hag for Bipin? Why waste such a gifted boy with someone like her? Surely there isn't a drought of good decent girls in Bengal?"

In the midst of all that newness, homesickness, and attacks on her parents and family, I imagine Basantamayi sought the comfort of familiar objects. I imagine her tucked in a corner of the puja room, cloaked in the faint scent of sandalwood, the fading glow of the sun lighting up the faces of the gods and goddesses. I wonder if she reread her favorite stories from Hindu mythology, the ones in which the unjust are punished, and the devoted are blessed, praised, and raised to the heavens.

ॐ

My earliest memories of goddesses are from the year I turned four. A small temple, the size of a modest apartment, stood at the turn of our neighborhood in Calcutta. During the day, as I went back and forth from home to school accompanied by Ma or Baba or fed ducks in a nearby pond with my grandmother, the temple served as an identifying landmark, its dark interiors dimly visible from the street, and inside it, the goddess Kali shimmering like a shadow.

I would observe the priests, dressed in white cotton dhotis, their upper bodies bare, going about their daily chores and guarding the goddess from the rest of us. At night though, she glowed under the white lights of the ceiling, and in spite of the loud clamor of the brass bells, the blur from the hundred incense sticks, and the noisy traffic right outside the temple walls, her face was clearly visible and her eyes bored into mine: *I see you*, they would warn, until I would break contact and look away.

Ma said the goddess was watching over me because every minute of every day she saw everything and everyone. That sentiment, meant to comfort, did exactly the opposite. It made me uncomfortable. I didn't want to be watched all the time. I wanted to be left alone to play my games, observe the neighbors, and make up stories about them in my head.

It was also Ma who taught me to pray. "Bring your hands together, yes, like that, dip your head a little, that's the right way to do nomoshkar. Ask the goddess to bless you." I did so without protest. I did so even though I didn't really understand the meaning of blessings or their purpose.

It was around this time that my grandfather presented me with a comic book that contained five stories, each featuring one of the hundreds and thousands of goddesses that make up the Hindu pantheon. The first story was about Durga, the mother goddess.

ॐ

I love that the story of Durga begins with a demon. His name is Mahishasura. He is a shapeshifter. He can turn himself into a buffalo at will. Mahishasura undergoes harsh penance to please Brahma, the god of creation. When Brahma appears before him and promises to grant him any boon he pleases, Mahishasura asks for immortality.

Brahma refuses. *Immortality is for the gods*, he says.

Mahishasura reconsiders. He makes another request: *Grant me the boon that I may not be killed by any man.*

Tathastu, says Brahma, *so be it.*

Mahishasura misunderstands the blessing. He

translates Brahma's words to mean he has attained immortality. To him, the idea of being killed by a woman is as laughable as it is impossible. Drunk on his new power, Mahishasura goes on a rampage. He kills innocents and destroys temples. He vanquishes kings and occupies kingdoms. Then he turns his attention toward the gods. So confident is he of victory that he marches toward the heavens. The gods panic. They call for a meeting. They combine their energies and from that infinite power, Durga is born. Her name means *the fortress*.

Each of her creators gives her a weapon. Ten arms, ten weapons. Shiva gifts her the trident, the chakra comes from Vishnu, so on and so forth. Thus armed, Durga sets out for Mahishasura. With her striking features, red sari, and gold ornaments, she is a stunning sight to behold. Mahishasura is so enraptured by her beauty that he offers her marriage. Durga smiles. She rejects him on account of her vow—she will only marry the man who can vanquish her in battle. Her words wound Mahishasura's ego, and he launches his fiercest attack on her. He tries to trick Durga by turning into a buffalo. The battle rages on until the moment Durga pierces his heart and restores peace on earth. It is this final dramatic moment of the story that is most loved and depicted by artists, and the context in which she was depicted on the cover of my comic book.

I still remember Durga in a green blouse and a red sari, her long wild hair billowing like smoke around her face. Her third eye was open, and her gold crown matched her numerous bracelets and necklace. She was astride her mount, a snarling lion with a thick mane. In each of her ten arms, she held weapons—lasso, snake, sword, mace, bow and arrow, and an axe. A thick stream of blood dripped from her scimitar. Mahishasur's skin was an unhealthy, blue-green color. Half of his body was in the shape of a man and the other that of a buffalo. He lay at Durga's feet. His eyes bulged and his neck, severed from the rest of his body, lay in a puddle of blood.

In spite of the ferociousness of the image, I don't remember being scared. Perhaps because the comic book was not my first introduction to Durga. By then, I had already seen her in calendars and wall art, in sculptures and icons in temples and shops, and inside people's homes, molded out of terracotta, marble and granite, Styrofoam, gold and silver. I loved it all—the fierce story, the powerful goddess, and the fairytale ending. I had no trouble in reposing my faith in any of these fantastic elements.

My questions began a few years later: "Why doesn't Durga answer back? Has anyone ever seen her talk? What does she sound like? What makes her different from the dolls I play with at home? Can I pray to them instead? How can you be so sure that those dolls are meant for play and Durga is for worship? How do you know she watches everyone and doesn't snooze away her afternoons?"

The older I got, the more I read, and the more cynical my questions became. By this time, thanks to my father's job, we had moved to New Delhi, and here, no matter how many times I accompanied my mother to the temple, I refused to bow my head.

I clung to one Hindu ritual, but the rest I quietly discarded. This, too, had been taught to me by my mother. As a child, if I ever dropped a book or a notebook or a writing instrument, Ma told me to pick it up, touch it to my head, then heart, and ask for its forgiveness. She taught me that Saraswati, the goddess of learning in Hinduism, lives inside every article of education. As a child, this explanation made complete sense. As I grew older, so did its metaphorical meaning.

I also continued to participate in Durga Puja, the multi-day festival held every autumn to honor the goddess Durga. To anyone who asked, I said, "I am a social Hindu." Fortunately, I was not alone. In India, Durga Puja is probably one of those festivals that draws everyone irrespective of their faith or lack thereof. It offers an excellent time to connect with friends, family, and neighbors, splurge on gifts and new clothes, and indulge in traditional foods too decadent for the rest of the year.

ॐ

I imagine the significance of Durga Puja must have been even greater during Basantamayi's lifetime, when there were limited entertainment opportunities, when the frenzied devotion to sports and cinema hadn't replaced the need and dependence on organized religion. I imagine that my great-grandmother looked forward to Durga Puja even more than the village priests did. Cloistered otherwise within the home, the festival offered an opportunity to travel—so what if the venue was the zamindar's mansion located less than ten minutes away? It gave her, and others like her, the chance to observe village life, to meet other women, to laugh, giggle, comment on each other's clothing and jewelry, eat food cooked by someone else, and to watch plays and performances in spite of jostling for space behind a screen. Surely, the cumulative total of these experiences was priceless. They afforded my great-grandmother an escape from daily chores, especially in her large joint family where guests stayed for weeks, sometimes months. Granted, the chores were not hers alone but were shared by other women; still, an opportunity to escape their daily drudgery must have been spectacular.

I wonder if on those days, when she eyed the shrine of Dugra, it thrilled Basantamayi to see balding wizened men bowing their heads to a young beautiful woman. Did it please Basantamayi that they fasted in Durga's honor and sang hymns in her praise?

ॐ

It wasn't until I left India for Idaho that I had to scrutinize my own position on Durga. Neither my secularism nor dismissal of faith had prepared me for my university students' questions. The first time I pulled up an image of Durga to talk about Hindu iconography, my students gawked. "That is scary," a blonde young woman whispered from the front row. Three men, from a couple of rows behind her, said something under their breaths and burst into giggles. A fourth, the intellectual of the class, raised his hand politely. When I nodded, he cleared his throat elaborately, paused for dramatic effect and asked, "Professor, what *is* this?"

It shocked me to discover how much my students' stares and jabs stung, how close I came to tears. It was as if I had allowed a beloved family member to be disrobed in front of a mob, and I was a mute bystander, a mere witness to relentless judgment and scrutiny of her person. Later, as I left campus, it occurred to me that in my offended state, I had ignored some genuinely smart and profound questions. For example, the anthropology major had asked if female priests assumed primary roles during Durga Puja. I had said, "No," and to her follow-up question, "Why not?" I had been unable to deliver a suitable answer.

In all the years I had attended Durga Puja, I had seen women perform only secondary roles. They assisted the male priests. They cut fruits for the worship ceremony. They lit the incense. They held trays and passed them from one hand to the other. They blew conch shells. But they did not recite the classical Sanskrit mantras dedicated to the goddess. That power, that authority, lived in the vocal chords of men. I had always accepted that as normal. But now, thanks to my student, I was forced to confront the "normalcy" of a female-centric festival controlled and operated by men. Clearly, I had much to learn about my own faith.

I remember I didn't go straight home that evening. I went to my favorite café instead, where the humdrum of small town Americana unfolded around me. I pulled up Durga's most ubiquitous image on my laptop. Across from me, a middle-aged woman in a turquoise shirt tap-tap-tapped on her MacBook, pausing occasionally to rub the ring on her wedding finger. On my left, a muscular guy dressed in black sweatpants, cap, and sweatshirt, and with tattoos on the backs of both his hands, talked to his friends, all of them white and muscular and equally tattooed. At a table behind me, two girls chatted giddily about their new boyfriends. I stared at Durga's image. For the first time in my life, I saw her through the eyes of others. I counted all her "weird" features: the third eye, the ten arms, the waging of a battle from the back of a lion.

In the end, my research turned out to be a useful exercise because it dredged up a long-forgotten memory of the first time I saw an image of Christ. I must have been about six years old and had only recently been admitted to St. Anthony's, the Catholic school I would attend for twelve years of my life. Like thousands of similar parents, mine, too, wanted me to be educated in an environment of discipline and austerity. The sight of the scrawny man on the cross, bleeding and so obviously in pain, was horrifying as was the gradual realization that in my school, there was no escaping him. He was everywhere. He stared at me inside classrooms, from various pieces of wall art, and from the rings and necklaces the nuns wore with pride.

I closed my laptop. I thought of words such as *contexts* and *perspectives*. The next morning, I checked out an armload of books from the university library. I had to learn to defend Durga.

ಲ

Durga is what is called a "composite goddess." She has one hundred and eight names. Each of these names is layered with complexity and meaning and contains myths of its own. While no one can pinpoint the exact date of Durga's creation nor the hour when she was worshipped for the first time, this much can be safely ventured: her origins were tribal; she was worshipped by fringe populations who revered a mother goddess figure; and the process of her transformation from a forest/tribal goddess into one firmly established in the Hindu cannon, where she came to be worshipped by millions, took centuries. As Devdutt Pattnaik points out in *Devi: The*

Mother Goddess, before urbanization and the stifling influence of civilization, humanity depended on earthy mother goddesses for hope and nourishment. They tied their object of veneration with elements drawn from the plant and animal world. There was the heron-faced Bagalamukhi, the turtle-riding Yamuna, the crocodile-riding Ganga, and Gayatri, the radiant goddess borne of a cow, among others. But the move out of the forest toward urban centers and a more settled form of life pushed people to move away from earthy divinity and look skyward in search of a father god.

During the autumnal festival held in her honor, Durga is worshipped in nine different forms, one form for each day until she is immersed in water on the tenth day so that she may undergo the cycle of renewal and rebirth that lies at the heart of Hinduism. The range of complexities within these nine forms is astonishing. While on the one hand, she is Mahagauri, the dressed-in-white, icon-of-purity; on the other, she is Kaalratri, the violent and vengeful form. She is Shailaputri, the daughter of the mountains and metaphorically, a source of strength and spiritual standing, but also Brahmacharini, the hermitess who inspires her devotees to lead simple lives. Chandraghanta is the warrior whose bell, shaped like a half-moon, strikes fear in the hearts of her enemies, and through Siddhidaatri, she fulfills her devotee's aspirations.

༄

This is a story I heard from my grandfather:

In 1948, Basantamayi became a mother-in-law for the fourth time. Her oldest daughter and her two sons had all gotten married in the last few years and had gifted her with a few grandchildren. This time it was her youngest son, my grandfather, who was about to be married. But unlike his older siblings, he had done it all wrong. He had secretly married a so-called low-caste girl of his choice in Calcutta, the nearest big city where they had ostensibly gone to pursue education. My grandfather's actions so enraged Basantamayi that she bolted herself inside her room. She howled and beat her chest, and when the newlyweds arrived to take her blessings, she wailed to the skies, the way one might berate the universe after losing a child. She couldn't imagine living with the shame her youngest son had brought upon his family. How could he do this? How could he sacrifice dignity for love?

When I first heard the story, I was fifteen and easily outraged. I couldn't imagine a wedding causing so much grief. When I think of that incident now, I picture Basantamayi locked inside her room, beating her fists against a heavy mahogany bed, her uncombed hair a spiderweb on her face. She hears snatches of conversation filtering in from other parts of her home as the family nervously prepares to receive the newlyweds. Someone sets up trays of rice and vermillion, another lights incense sticks and earthen lamps, a third decorates the threshold with garlands of marigolds and mango leaves, all of them trying to follow some semblance of the rituals, even though they know these duties are not rightfully theirs. These are to be performed by the matriarch of the family.

∞

Over the years, I have come to realize that telling and retelling the story of Durga brings me great joy, especially if I am doing so inside an American classroom, where female students say "sorry" almost nonstop. They say sorry to me and to everyone else. They do so irrespective of whether it's a freshman class with thirty-five students or an upper division honors course with fifteen. They apologize when I meet them in smaller groups for conferences, and when they stop by my office. If two students start answering the same question at the same time, inevitably, it is the female student who apologizes and looks stricken, as if somehow she has crossed a line and ventured into an inviolate space where her presence is unwelcome. I have personally interceded several times to ensure they don't prefix their questions or sentences with "sorry." Once, a student apologized to me for no fault of her own but because I misspelled her name.

I tell my students that one of Durga's greatest strengths is her unapologetic nature. When I was four and learning about Durga, I had no concept or understanding of feminism. But because iconography is the study of symbols and meanings, I want to think that nearly three thousand years ago, at the time of the creation of her mythology, some Hindus did. The fact that she owes her creation to male energies is not unusual. Think Eve. Think Athena stepping out of Zeus' head, fully-grown and dressed in armor, when the smith-god Hephaistos cracks it open with an axe.

I want to uphold the image of Durga as deeply feministic. I want to present her to my students as yet another face of feminism. Time and again, I have seen them hold the same stereotypical image of feminists— they must be hairy; they must be lesbians averse to fine clothes, jewelry, and makeup; and hateful toward men, families, and stay-at-home moms. I want them to know feminist icons don't have to be white. They can be red sari-clad and with oodles of jewelry. So what if they are fantastic and mythical?

Recently, one of my female students wrote an essay on how the story of Durga has emboldened her to not hold herself back in her engineering classes, where she is one of a mere handful of female students. I look upon this, the relevance of an ancient goddess from the mountains of north India straight into a 21st century classroom in northern Idaho, as a small but important victory.

In India, Durga's influence is not merely relegated to mythology or once-a-year-veneration of her prowess. Her influence shines through in folklore, in contemporary art, and architecture. In cinema, she features either as a character or a metaphor: case in point, the Hindi film *Mardaani*. Released in 2014, it stars the powerhouse performer Rani Mukherji, essaying the role of a cop fighting a child-trafficking mafia. The title *Mardaani* means *manlike* and is a salutation used for Durga.

Sadly, our veneration of the powerful goddess does not eliminate our hypocrisy. While on the one hand, Indian women continue to take huge strides in government, education, and private sectors, such as banking and communication, the country still suffers from high rates of female infanticide, the culture of rape and dowry, and the inescapable hold of patriarchy in every aspect of life. Which is why, as Wendy Doniger notes in her controversial book *The Hindus*, "...the more powerful the goddess, the less power for real women." In 2013, the Mumbai-based ad agency Taproot was commissioned by

NGO Save the Children India to run a campaign against domestic abuse and female trafficking. It was unnerving to see iconic images of Hindu goddesses—while still beautifully adorned in gold jewelry and rich saris and bearing a plethora of sacred symbols, like conches, lotuses, and tridents—recreated with black eyes, split lips, and bloodied noses.

ॐ

These days, I find myself less outraged by my great-grandmother Basantamayi's actions. I remember what little say she had in terms of her own life and future, and the ease with which she was transferred like a commodity from her father to her husband. I count the things I know about her—she was very hospitable as long as the guests were high-caste Hindus, and she maintained a separate set of hookahs, plates, and cups for Muslim visitors for fear of pollution. We are separated from each other by only two generations, and yet, our differences could fill up a room. By age fifteen, Basantamayi was not just a wife, she was also a mother. She was still deeply wedded to her gods and goddesses. By the time I was fifteen, I had lost all inclination for prayer. I had dated two boys, gotten drunk, smoked a few cigarettes, bunked school, excelled and cheated in exams, and introduced comparatively innocent friends to porn.

I wonder if in her mind, Basantamayi assumed that just like the mothers in Hindu mythology, she, too, would command the unquestioning respect of her children and they would give her the dignity she never received as a wife or daughter, obeying her just the way she had obeyed her elders at age ten.

In her powerful essay, "What We Hunger For," Roxane Gay writes, "I am always interested in the representations of strength in women, where that strength comes from, how it is called upon when it is needed most, and what it costs for a woman to be strong. All too often, representations of a woman's strength overlook that cost." I wonder—was Basantamayi's grief and outright rejection of her new daughter-in-law an expression of strength? By denying her grief, did her family members deny her the agency to negotiate the world on her own terms?

I remember the outrage I felt when I learned how Basantamayi had humiliated my grandparents when they were newlyweds. But are Basantamayi and I really all that different? We both acted out defensively when repositories of our affection, deeply personal to us yet absurd to others, were attacked or we felt were under attack. How could we withstand their debunking? Which makes me wonder if in insisting that my female students follow my understanding of strength, I am denying them their own model of strength, the codes they must create to understand, shape, and engage with their world. After all, Durga, too, is not one single entity. She has one hundred and eight names.

In time, I learned from my grandfather that Basantamayi did overcome the resentment she felt against his wife, her youngest daughter-in-law. She came to love her grandson, my father. And she continued to love stories for as long as she lived. Meanwhile, I remain an atheist by faith, a Hindu in name and on officious-looking forms, and do not believe there are ten-armed goddesses hovering in the sky. Yet every time I drop a notebook or a book or a pencil, I pick it up with reverence, I touch it to my forehead, and plead for forgiveness. I remind students what an incredible gift it is to be in college, inside a classroom. I tell them my story of being scared by the image of Christ on a cross, and I repeat the words "context" and "perspective" again and again so they remember not to dismiss someone's objects of veneration and affection as "weird."

Inside my apartment, Durga continues to live on in small tokens: a bookmark with the image of her third eye, a poster of a film in which she appears as a theme, a handful of books exploring the meaning behind her myths and icons, and occasional doodles on top of newspaper headlines. I hold her gaze the way a devotee might at the temple, mirroring the concept of Darsan or sacred sight in Hinduism, whose intended purpose is so the Divine may bless the recipient. We lock eyes until I break contact and look away.

Why Home is a Bad Bollywood Movie

On a late November evening in Moscow, Idaho, my boyfriend and I are on our way to dinner. I have requested that it be at our local Thai restaurant because that's the closest thing I can get to Indian food in our tiny university town. I can already taste the explosion of fish sauce, duck meat, peppers, pineapple, and basil. They are a fine compensation on this evening the color of ash and peat, the skeletal limbs of the trees signaling the imminent arrival of unrelenting snow.

Inside the car, I press play on my iPhone. A rhythmic Sanskrit chant bursts open accompanied by the heady beats of *dhol*. The robust and powerful song roars. It fills up the car. It is the title track of *Singham*, literally "the lion," a Bollywood movie about an honest cop and the obstacles he must overcome in his quest for justice. The summer I last visited India, I heard this song everywhere—on radio stations and cell phones, at grocery stores and Punjabi restaurants, inside people's homes and at the local gym, where elderly housewives sprinted to it in billowy salwar kameezes.

I close my eyes, lean back against the seat, and *Singham* blurs it all: this university town where I arrived as a student then stayed on to teach, the piles of essays I must grade by tonight, the scrawny trees lining the sidewalk, and my acute longing for Thai food. Effortlessly, the song transports me back to New Delhi, particularly to its winters, and I taste the wood smoke and fog, those barely visible skies, and scalding-hot chai accompanied by spicy cauliflower pakoras.

When we pull into the restaurant's parking lot, I murmur, "I miss Ajay Devgan. I really do."

My boyfriend narrows his eyes but doesn't say anything. He is Indian-American. His parents arrived here years before his birth. He watched Hindi films growing up, but the name Ajay Devgan does not mean to him what it means to me. I imagine his mind sifting through Devgan's films we have watched together. Finally, he gives up. "Why?" he asks.

৳০

Imagine this:

Two motorbikes—one red, the other blue. Their well-oiled bodies, taut like racehorses, gleam under the bright sunlight. Their helmetless riders vroom down the asphalt, setting off swirling clouds of dust. You hear the engines bellowing like monsters, although nothing can be heard over the loud guitar riff in the background.

You ignore the riders and focus instead on a third man. Dressed in black jeans, black t-shirt, and a tan jacket, he has firmly planted one foot on each of the motorbike's seats. His broad shoulders, aviator sunglasses, and proud bearing confirm what you already suspect: he is a badass.

The road is flanked on both sides by boys and girls, his adoring friends and fans. The boys cheer and wave, and the girls—in shiny oversized skirts, typical of 1990s Indian fashion—blow him kisses. He jauntily acknowledges the love, then balances himself atop the motorbikes via a well-executed split, accentuating his badass-ness.

This epic hero is none other than the actor Ajay Devgan essaying the role of an angry young man in his debut-making Bollywood blockbuster *Phool aur Kaante* (*Flowers and Thorns*). Released in 1991, the motorbike scene, in particular, highlighted his height, fitness, and obvious machismo, leaving many women across India weak-kneed and breathless, thus setting the stage for several decades of Devgan's enduring popularity.

That same year, I got myself my very first boyfriend, D. He and I were both twelve and we met one afternoon when I was doing lazy figure-eights with my bicycle on a narrow stretch of concrete, and he, standing a few feet away, was tossing a lime-green tennis ball against a brick wall.

Although it had been a year since my family had moved into this neighborhood, I was still very much the new kid. I kept mostly to myself, opting for long, solo bike rides or walks with my brother to avoid appearing in desperate need of friends. The few kids my age I knew, I didn't care for, such as the girl next door whose favorite pastime involved cataloguing and re-cataloguing her enormous collection of hair clips and earrings, or the spoilt-brat boy who dated the spoilt-brat girl of our neighborhood, or the three thirteen-year-olds who called themselves, "the three beauties."

That first afternoon when D initiated conversation, he wore a brown t-shirt over blue jeans, and his thick shaggy hair hung in an arc over his face. He was not the best-looking boy, but he was tall for his age and had wide shoulders, a sharp nose, and a strong jawline. He reminded me of Ajay Devgan.

D pursued me, in the most romantic sense possible, for nearly a month. He played footsie with me under the table. He wanted to go on long walks. He declared that he would rather spend every evening with me than with anyone else. His attention was by far the most exciting thing that had ever happened to me. And so we began to date. But in secret. Because back in 1991, good Indian girls didn't date. And certainly not at age twelve.

I was too young to realize it then, but 1991 was a special year. It was one of change, not just for me but for the country as a whole. Only recently, India had opened its shores to economic liberalization, and we were on our way to golden-arched restaurants selling happy meals and western cola giants fighting to quench our tropical thirst. Inside our homes though, we were still being raised with "wholesome Indian values," one of which was no dating, at least not until college.

Our first few dates are still fresh in my memory. It was October and D and I found alibis to cover for us while we utilized the surrounding urban sprawl—empty garages, abandoned stores, and parks long after the sun had set and the children had gone home. That's where we learned to kiss clumsily and with fear, knowing with every breath how angry our parents would be if they found out, and how much of a scandal it would cause in our neighborhood. But we didn't stop. The thrill alone was enough encouragement.

Soon, however, an unexpected problem reared its head. What came after the kissing and the making out? I felt confused, torn between the duty of staying Indian while desiring to become cool, which meant *American*, whose very different standards of coolness were now being beamed into our homes. I didn't have an older sibling to lay down the law or discuss protocol. And of course, talking to parents, whether mine or someone else's, was simply out of the question.

So for better or worse, I turned to Bollywood. Surely something in there would teach me the rules. But that turned out to be disappointing. For one, the characters were all older and routinely broke into impossible songs and dances. Sure, the girls wore western clothes on screen, but because they were all good and virtuous, they always upheld Indian values and tripped over themselves to serve as sacrificial lambs for any cause they deemed suitable, whether it benefitted their families, their beloveds, or best friends—anything requiring a touch of sentiment. The bad girls lived at the other extreme. They were identifiable by their almost biological need to smoke, drink, show cleavage, and steal boyfriends.

I understood that I was on my own. Which is perhaps why, once routine settled in, my great romance fizzled out. It lasted only three months, simply because beyond a point, I didn't know what to do with a boyfriend.

&

A lot has changed in the decades since Ajay Devgan straddled those two motorbikes and roared into my life and into India's collective consciousness with panache. I have migrated to America, and this new landscape has seeped into me in unexpected ways: I know the difference between a venti and a grande at Starbucks, I fiendishly protect my "personal bubble," I greet people with "how's it going" and wish them "have a good one" without breaking my stride.

My family doesn't live in that neighborhood anymore, so I don't know what's happened to D, my first boyfriend, the boy who once reminded me of Ajay Devgan. I wonder if he still bears that resemblance and what he remembers of our time together. Was it just another hormone-crazed winter? Like me, did he also seek out Bollywood for inspiration? Does he realize now that we were on the brink of change, not just in our own puny lives but in the ways our country transformed from the one we were born into?

I am not addicted to Ajay Devgan's movies. I never was. Yet, these days when I chance upon one or hear its music, it's as comforting as going home, as thrilling as meeting an old love, someone with whom I can share a half-smile, a quick kiss, an inside joke that we can't and won't tell others. It reminds me of that rush of adrenaline, of how my heart thumped when I returned home every evening, fearful my secret had been found out. And it makes me ache not just for New Delhi and its winters, but for that twelve-year-old girl who sneaked out every evening, desperate to be bad.

With Love to Captain Nemo

"The sea is everything. . . the embodiment of a supernatural and wonderful existence. It is nothing but love and emotion; it is the 'Living Infinite.'"

—Captain Nemo
Twenty Thousand Leagues Under the Sea

On my ninth birthday, I received Jules Verne's *Twenty Thousand Leagues under the Sea*, its briny adventures an unexpected gift for a girl growing up in the concrete landlocked jungle of New Delhi, nearly two thousand kilometers from the nearest ocean. I still remember the thrill of reading this sentence: "With its untold depths, couldn't the heart of the ocean hide the last–remaining varieties of these titanic species for whom years are centuries and centuries millennia?" Those words presented deliciously exciting and yet frightening possibilities, and I felt clamped to the pages by phantom tentacles. After that, it took all kinds of self-control to set the book aside and do boring things like eat, sleep, and go to school.

Like any good adventure story, *Twenty Thousand Leagues under the Sea* begins with a mystery wherein the French biologist Professor Aronnax, the Canadian harpooner Ned, and the professor's servant Conseil are on a quest to discover the powerful monster causing havoc in the world's oceans. They are soon captured by the "monster," which turns out to be the submarine *Nautilus*, built and helmed by its enigmatic leader, Captain Nemo.

As I read and reread the book, I was stunned that this world, replete with ink-squirting squids, underground cemeteries, and deep-sea pearl divers was the product of one person's imagination. And his name was Jules Verne, a man with an imagination so powerful that he bequeathed to his readers an endless supply of ingenuity and inventiveness. I remember the introduction stating that at the time of the novel's publication, European scientists were barely producing sparks of electricity in their laboratories, and here was Verne preposterously imagining running the *Nautilus* on it.

But what most captured my imagination was Nemo, the captain of the submarine. His name in Latin means "nobody." It is most befitting because at their first meeting, Professor Aronnax cannot be sure of the Captain's ethnic background, except that he is from a "low latitude" country such as Spain, Turkey, or India. His accent is hard to place because he switches seamlessly between multiple languages. He is a man of many talents. Not only has he designed and built the *Nautilus*, he owns and knows intimately the prodigious library on board. He is a scientist and an oceanographer. He writes with a quill pen made of whalebone, its ink the secretion of a squid, and his mattress comes from the "softest eelgrass."

But in spite of his many achievements, he insists he is not a "civilized man." As Professor Aronnax discovers, and through him so does the reader, Captain Nemo is defined by contradictions. He is wealthy yet feels for the poor. He is ruthless but funds revolutions against totalitarian regimes. He does not *obey laws* yet creates them. His only identity is his love for the sea because the sea cannot belong to tyrants. And yet, he himself *is* one. The Professor, Ned, and Conseil are his prisoners, but he treats them well. He provides them with sumptuous meals—procured fresh from the sea—and access to the dazzling life underwater and to his private library.

In the books I had read up to that point, irrespective of whether they were in English, Hindi, or Bengali, the division between the good characters and the bad had almost always been clear. But Captain Nemo was not like that. The line separating his good side from his bad was blurred. On the one hand, he was a villain because he sunk ships. However, he used the wealth of these ships to help overthrow cruel regimes. He killed people, especially if they represented colonizing governments, but also spared lives and treated his prisoners like honored guests. So who was he really, the good guy or the bad?

I finally made sense of him by identifying him with Arjuna, a hero of the *Mahabharata*, my other favorite book and one of India's ancient epics. In the final battlefield of his life, Arjuna faces his enemies with a heavy heart. His enemies are not strangers, after all. They are his cousins, uncles, and gurus. But his charioteer and mentor, Krishna, reminds him of his duty and how he is honor bound to do what is right and face up to evil. So what if it takes a toll on his conscience? I understood that Captain Nemo, too, had a similar burden to bear.

There was another significant way in which *Twenty Thousand Leagues* was different from the other books of my childhood. Those books tended to have monochromatic characters, either all Indian or all white. Although I didn't yet have a concept of race nor did I possess any tools of analysis, somewhere at the back of my mind, I may have noted that in this story it was the brown man, the odd outsider, who was the most assertive and compelling character in an otherwise sea of white.

Although Captain Nemo can be seen as a symbol of colonial rebellion and an echo of Verne's own tumultuous political views, to me, he was my first exposure to the idea of living one's life driven by passion, not being just another number in a herd. I have been supported in this idea by my parents, who unlike most middle-class parents in India, gave me as much freedom and as many choices as they gave my brother. I graduated with bachelors and masters degrees from top universities and then followed up by working for various publishing houses. But when life seemed like it was missing something, I quit a stable career track to follow my passion. I became a grad student in creative writing in far-flung, snowy Idaho.

It's only recently that I have learned that *Twenty Thousand Leagues* was also my father's favorite book when *he* was a child. He heard the story from his home tutor much before he could read it on his own. I imagine the scene: Baba, barely five years old, working his way through the day's lesson with thinly disguised anticipation, his heart willing the clock to move toward the last fifteen minutes of the hour. That was the bewitching hour, when his mustachioed tutor would narrate to him yet another chapter from *Twenty Thousand Leagues*. When I asked Baba for his favorite parts, he said, "The submarine and all the science." How telling that he became an engineer. I wonder if Captain Nemo's passion for the Nautilus influenced my father's career path. I also wonder if Verne could have imagined that nearly a hundred years after he wrote his masterpiece, his words would have such an impact on a father and daughter, far, far away in India?

I now live oceans and continents away from my parents. But I have developed book routines with my partner, also a brown-bearded man from the "southern latitudes." When we travel, we seek out libraries and bookstores and think nothing of the fact that books are always our greatest splurge. One summer, we vacationed at the foot of a lighthouse in a tiny Californian village called Point Arena. At dawn, we walked along the craggy shoreline and stared at the treacherous waters that the lighthouse keeper said had claimed many ships in the last century. I thought of Captain Nemo, and later that day, I wrote a strange improbable story. I think Verne would have approved.

My Grandfather's Red Chair

One of my earliest memories of my grandfather is the two of us sitting side-by-side in identical red chairs in the drawing room of his home in Calcutta. I do not remember the first conversation we ever had, but I imagine we held hands, a system we followed everywhere—while taking evening walks in the neighborhood, or an overnight bus ride to the beach, or sitting through tedious hours of someone's wedding. In spite of the others who were with us—my parents, my grandmother, or my brother—he and I always sat together, and we always, always held hands.

Which is why, the night he passed away, my first reaction was not grief but an acute sense of betrayal. I screamed at him as I stormed through my apartment in rage, pausing only to punch my laptop keyboard rabidly while I searched for plane tickets from Spokane, Washington, to Calcutta, India. I couldn't log into the travel website because my name, too, is his gift: *Sayantani*, meaning *twilight* or *dusk* in Sanskrit, to mark the precise hour of my birth. I raged at him inside my head, "How dare you? It's the middle of the week, for heaven's sake. I can't just leave my students and classes and take off for you. How dare you go away without assuring me you have told me every story: *Have you really told me every story? Have you told it to me enough times so I will remember the details? What if I forget dates, names, places, or punchlines? What then?*"

∞

It's been more than two years since his death, and I still search for clues, wondering if he said goodbye to me in some subtle way, and I was too busy grading tests or reading *Buzzfeed* on my phone to notice. A part of me thinks that he should have tried harder and left me an actual message, a final tangible token of his love. Something more appropriate than a phrase like, "I love you" because "I love you" doesn't translate well in Bengali. It sounds ridiculous and silly, embarrassing even. Not once in my life did my grandfather ever tell me he loved me. It's just not the Bengali way of life. But he showed his love, talking to me like my opinion mattered even when I was a child, like I was his equal; when he composed nonsensical songs with me when I was four, and we sang them loudly and shamelessly in front of any audience we could find; and when he took me to museums and bookstores; and as I grew older, quizzing me on subjects like politics, religion, literature, and history, demanding that I defend my answers with logic and example, not childish sentimentality. It didn't matter whether his question was about the nature of British rule in India or why I preferred oranges over apples. When someone makes you the nucleus of his life, you find yourself willing and ready to follow him down every rabbit hole.

My favorite memory of my grandfather is from the summer I turned seven. My mother and I had just spent several weeks in Calcutta and on our last day, she and I were at the railway station about to board the train that would bring us back to New Delhi. We were surrounded by grandmothers, aunts, and uncles who had come to see us off. Everyone was accounted for except my grandfather.

Just as I was beginning to get irritated, he sauntered down the platform, his right hand holding up a neat arrangement of seven books stacked in a pile, bound together with brown twine. He handed them to me as an early birthday present, and I quickly did the math.

Seven books for my seven years on this planet, seven books for the next seven days of the week, seven books for the first seven hours of the train trip, only to be reread again before reaching New Delhi. I abandoned the math when the next few minutes became a blur of hugs, tears, and smiles from everyone. As the train jerked out of the wet-rag humidity that is Calcutta and began charging toward the dry, desert-like air of New Delhi, I understood that something incredible had just happened. I had received an extraordinary gift from an extraordinary man. He had taken the time to go to a bookstore and pick seven titles that would entertain not just any seven-year-old girl, but specifically *his* seven-year-old granddaughter who did not want to read stories of princesses, cutesy animals, or lost chickens but of haunted houses, vengeful ghosts, and witches with no feet. In that moment, I knew this was a man who would love me forever.

℘

My grandfather was born on February 3, 1926, in village Fatehabad, district Chittagong, in present-day Bangladesh, which back then was part of India and under the firm control of the British Crown. His parents named him Asit Ranjan, meaning "tranquil." As a boy, he was scrawny and not very popular among his peers. He did not share their enthusiasm for pranks. He was already a poet, far more interested in words and their meanings as they clustered and collided in his head. He spent most of his free time sprawled on the floor of his father's library, stocked with books written in three languages: classical

Sanskrit, Bengali, and English. He was close to his father, an erudite man who worked for the Salt and Excise Department of the British Government. But he received little attention from his mother, a devout woman who anchored her life to the gods and goddesses of the Hindu pantheon to such an extent that she never got to know her own children.

The village had a population of about ten thousand people. It had its own railway station, post office, a busy marketplace, a renowned library, and a coeducational school, the very concept of which was revolutionary at that time. This is where my grandfather first saw my grandmother, one of only four girls whose families thought it appropriate to educate their daughters.

Beginning in his childhood, several factors turned my grandfather into a skeptic and set in motion his journey toward a life of rationality. There was his own mother's excessive religiosity coupled with the superstitions that abounded in the village. (There were any number of ghosts haunting the neighboring ponds and trees.) Then there was the control exercised by the village council, comprised of a handful of ancient Brahmin men, who may or may not have read the scriptures carefully. And finally, there was his own research and dedicated scholarship. He read every holy book in the world, thought they contained entertaining stories, but for whatever Truth was out there, he firmly turned toward himself.

Once when he was seven years old, he was ordered by the same village council to atone for his sins by bowing to a cow and seeking its forgiveness. His sin? He had not only entered the home of his best friend, another seven-year-old boy, who happened to belong to a so-called lower caste, but he had consumed the lunch cooked by his friend's mother. The council was furious. Didn't Asit know any better than to pollute his own high caste by eating food cooked by a low-caste woman? How could he defile himself and his family? How dare he show such blatant disregard for the rules?

But my grandfather refused the council's dictates. He thought it downright silly to ask for an animal's forgiveness, particularly one as uninteresting as the cow, and he said so, much to the council's horror.

He wore this rationality like an armor all his life— when he married my grandmother for love and against the wishes of his family because they belonged to two different castes. When he married her in court and without the blessing of any religious authority. When he gave away his daughter, my aunt, in marriage but eschewed traditional Hindu injunctions that suggest a woman can be transferred, almost like a commodity, from her father to her husband. When he gave wise counsel to all those, both within our immediate family and outside, who came seeking his help, and he told them what was right and what they needed to hear, unclouded by sentiment. When he treated me, his granddaughter, the way I imagine most grandfathers treat their grandsons, and I learned from him not just the history of our family but a worldview that emphasized learning and education. He taught me the fundamental truth that my dreams and aspirations are just as valid as any man's.

But his unwavering faith in himself imparted my grandfather with a god-complex, and the red chair he favored in the drawing room almost became his throne. He didn't take kindly to criticism and handed down to his children and grandchildren the same superiority complex, a sense that our family's education and scholarly pursuits, our disdain for excessive religiosity, made us better than most people around us and that our way of looking at the world was not only right but the only one acceptable. This inherited belief system has challenged me, particularly now that I live in the American West, where I have encountered a feverish deification for the ability to work and build with one's hands and a parallel dismissive attitude toward intellectualism. I particularly see this at the university where I teach when students offer their opinion, holding it to be as good as fact. It is at those moments that I picture my grandfather inside my classroom, and I wonder how poorly he would have fared in the current climate of political correctness, how easily he would have ignored the voices he didn't deem intelligent, how quickly he would have tired of all those who say, "I don't know," when they don't want to venture an opinion for fear of appearing aggressive.

Sometimes, when I think of my grandfather's world view, I uncharitably wonder how strong our relationship would have been had I lived all or most of my life under the same roof with him, in the manner of most joint families in India. Were we inseparable because we saw each other only for a couple of weeks every year, relying otherwise on letters and phone calls to sustain our conversation? If the three generations of our family had indeed lived together, I imagine I would have chafed at his rules. He may have insisted on the kind of friends I should have, the glittering report cards I should bring back from school, the sophisticated Bengali music I should listen to, or the flawless way I should conduct myself in public because my behavior would be a constant reflection of my family.

I also wonder about the amount of independence my parents would have had within that traditional framework. Would they have been able to make all decisions with respect to raising my brother and me or would they have had to defer to my grandparents? Would my mother have been able to truly and openly voice her opinions? Or would she have been forced to suppress ideas that challenged the boundaries set for the ever-dutiful daughter-in-law? Would my father have lived in worry that his own children might see their grandfather as more of a role model than him? And would my grandfather have really been proud of me taking his rules and techniques but applying them in my own way to my life, especially during those years when I didn't want to study, when I didn't want to be a good student, when I wanted to be left alone to chase the many temptations teenage life had suddenly lit up for me? But these questions will forever remain unanswered. There is a system we follow in my family, and these questions are not a part of it.

I defied my grandfather once. I was twelve years old and it was a Saturday evening in Calcutta during another summer vacation. The following afternoon, we were expecting some guests over for lunch. My mother and grandmother were already busy in the kitchen. My father was out finishing some last minute shopping. My grandfather and I were in the drawing room, in our identical red chairs, when I told him that I didn't see the merit behind the Hindu system of greeting one's elders by bending down to the waist, touching their feet with the right hand, and bringing it back to the forehead, thus symbolically conveying, *the dust of your feet will bless me*. "People's feet are gross," I said. "I don't believe I should respect someone older simply on account of their age or because I am tied to them by blood. For me to touch someone's feet, they would have to earn my respect first."

My grandfather's eyes hardened. He did not shout because that would be unseemly. But in a steely voice that I can still hear, he reminded me that some of the guests were older than him. If he could touch their feet so could I. If he thought they were worthy of respect, then they were, and that should be good enough for me.

But it wasn't. And I said so, which was akin to playing with fire because I had never heard anyone talk back to him. If my parents heard the exchange, I would be in serious trouble. But in that moment, my grandfather's logic seemed as irrational to me as the same Brahmins' he had once despised. If he could stand up to them, why was he denying me the opportunity to be rational? Why was his assurance that the guests were older and thus respectable the only guarantee I needed?

He remained aloof for the next several days, perhaps expecting an apology. But I didn't offer it then, I didn't offer it later, and I still don't offer it now.

๙

In spite of these doubts and questions, I haven't been to Calcutta since my grandfather passed away. Because if I don't go, I can pretend he is well. Perhaps he is in his bedroom, the curtains drawn against the sun, but the room still well-lit enough for him to prop himself against a mini-mountain of pillows, reading *The Statesman,* the newspaper he swore his loyalty to as a teenager and read every day of his life. Or perhaps he is in his red chair in the drawing room, correcting proofs of the literary journal he used to edit, a cup of tea idling on the table.

Last year, when my mother brought up the subject of my next visit, I hurriedly gave her a list of reasons why it's impossible for me to visit Calcutta in the summer. "Ma, I have too much to do in America. I have to attend multiple writing conferences. I am teaching at all of them. I have to finish writing my book. I have to prep for fall courses."

My mother, the wisest woman in the world, heard me quietly and said, "Even if you come ten years from now, he will still be gone."

In my mind, I constantly imagine my trip to Calcutta. I imagine landing at the airport and a taxi driving me through those familiar, wet-with-monsoons roads to my grandparents' home. Unlike other times, the drive will not take thirty minutes. It will be over in less than one suffocating, stomach-clenching moment. Usually, on my first day back, I breathe hungrily, as if I have learned how to distill the scent of dust, rain, heat, and spices in a vial inside me, and when I return to America, all I have to do is spritz it all over.

But this time, I know it will be different.

I won't devour all the writing in Bengali on billboards, hoardings, and movie posters. My ears won't soak up with gratitude and a whole lot of irritation from all that noise—goddammit we are a loud people—but how I have missed the mix of words in Hindi, English, Bengali, and a dozen other languages I don't know nor understand, the songs and jingles from passing cars and their radios, the piercing honks of buses and trucks, the pull and push that is true for any big city, and the cursing—loud, crude, and profane—without which driving in India is almost disrespectful.

But I will ignore it all.

Instead, I will swallow hard and talk very fast with whomever has come to pick me up, so as to not burst into tears. So as to not surprise or confuse the driver. So as to honor my grandfather by not making a sweeping emotional display in public.

The taxi will pull to a stop in front of the three-story house with a black gate and a marble letterbox that will still bear his name. I will open the gate and step in to the paved driveway, my ears missing the furious jangle of keys from the drawing room, followed by the cry, "Dadi, eshe gechhish?" "Granddaughter, are you here?"

This time, it will be my grandmother who opens the door, the same door he opened countless times—summer vacations, winter vacations, when I came visiting from my first job, heady from the newly-minted salary that allowed me to buy my grandmother an expensive sari, or when I stopped by before the first time I flew to half-a-world-away Idaho. Unlike other grandfathers who may have pummeled the souls of their grandchildren with sentimental tosh, mine joked, "Doesn't everyone address everyone by name in America? Does this mean when you come back, you will pretend we are the same age?"

I hope my grandmother will forgive my reaction at seeing her without the red vermilion in the parting of her hair, or when I clasp her wrists and notice they are missing the red coral and white conch shell bangles she wore for the sixty-four years that she was married to my grandfather. When I walk into the drawing room, I will see my grandfather's empty red chair. I will fill the identical one next to it as usual, but unlike my previous visits to

Calcutta, this time my hand won't automatically reach for my grandfather's, and his long slim fingers won't link with mine.

Fire Girl

Once, there was a girl made of fire. My mother read me her story when I was five. The fire girl's name was Draupadi, and when she stepped out of the flames, she was already a grown woman. Fire molded her limbs and left imprints as it crisscrossed through her still pliant, unblemished skin and burned into shape the ridges and furrows that became her eyes, nose, hands, and feet.

Draupadi's hair was thick as smoke. It was unruly and the color of soot. I imagined the hair framed her face unevenly because she neither braided it with ribbons or garlands nor tamed it with pins and clips. My copy of the *Mahabharata* said that Draupadi's skin was the color of dark chocolate but tinted and flecked as if with gold. I understood it to mean that fire always left traces.

"But didn't the flames hurt when Draupadi stepped out of them?" I asked. I knew from experience that fire hurt. Just on my last birthday, when I'd leaned forward over the chocolate cake to blow out the candles, while my friends and parents sang for me in the background, I had felt the monsoon wind that whooshes through New Delhi in July gather around me like an uninvited guest. It had swooped down on the flame of the fifth candle, making that little stick of light wobble and then topple on my finger. The flame singed my skin, and two drops of wax gleamed like bubbles on my hand then thickened like glue. They didn't make a single sound; they resembled teardrops, but pinched so much more. The bubbles merged and left a scar—a circle browner than the rest of my skin.

But my mother said, "Flames don't hurt fire girls and anything is possible in a story." She said "in a story" twice.

And I believed her.

When I was six, the owner of a toy store invited me to sit on his lap and play with a Barbie while his fingers made deft circles on my flat chest, as if willing my breasts to sprout by magic. Barbie wore white panties and the man asked me to show him if I were wearing white panties as well. I remember wanting the game to end. I remember asking for my mother. But the man said firmly, "Let me see your panties." Fearing punishment, I let him. I didn't understand why his dry bony finger kept going in and out of me or why his nail kept rubbing something that I didn't know I possessed.

At the time of her birth, the fire girl was named Krishnaa, the dark one. But all her life, and later when she became a character in a book, everyone called her Draupadi, *the daughter of* Drupad, the king of Panchala. At the time of her birth, a voice had cried out from the sky. It had proclaimed that Draupadi would cause a devastating war that would change the course of history. And she did. She hurt a man's ego, and there was war.

In spite of her notoriety, no one ever called her "the dark one." They only called her Draupadi, the name she acquired because of her association with her father. But King Drupad wasn't a fire child. His birth was normal and insignificant like the rest of us.

One afternoon when I was eleven, while walking back from school, a car crawled in close to me. The man inside drove slowly, as if his car were a fragile and vulnerable keepsake, as if one quick brake could shatter it into smithereens. I felt a sting on my right hip, a pinch from that man in the car. I spun around to take a good look at him. The shock must have shown on my face. He threw back his head and laughed. I remember staring at his fleshy gums and gapped teeth. He was a heavy smoker. I could smell it on his breath and see it in his mouth. His hand was inches away from where he had touched me. A sinuous silver bracelet was coiled to his wrist, and before I could react, he smacked the same spot again, a tight slap I can still hear, and drove away. This time, the car rushed past as if it couldn't wait to reach its next destination.

The same year, three friends and I spotted a man leaning in on one of the four gates of our girls-only school. We had been sitting and eating at our usual spot, a cemented bench that circled the base of a giant tree thick with dark green leaves, no matter the season. About two thousand girls were scattered all over our campus, eating the same kind of lunch, which is why this relatively secluded tree had been our special spot for the last two or so years.

We all noticed him at the same time. Maybe it was his thick mustache. Or because his contorted face was slick with sweat. Or maybe it was his panting. Or because his hands went up and down. Why was he stroking his *thing?* Why was he calling out to us? Why would we want to touch *it?* We ran away. Didn't he know we were not supposed to talk to strangers? I went home and complained to my mother.

At her insistence, the next day I reported the matter to our class teacher. Almost immediately, a guard was appointed to stroll the grounds and keep an eye out for possible miscreants. My friends and I were told to stay away from our tree-bench and congregate in one of the more crowded places on campus. As if it had somehow been the tree's fault. Or ours.

∞

By an accident of fate, Draupadi became the wife of not one, but five men.

All of them brothers.

All of them princes.

All of them married to her at the same time, and all of them with equal conjugal rights.

Yet all of them stood mute and helpless when Yudhishthir, the oldest and ironically the wisest of the five brothers, gambled her away in a game of dice. To celebrate, her new owner, a prince and a cousin to all of her five husbands, grabbed her by the hair and dragged her to a packed assembly, where he intended to humiliate her. He reasoned that because she was now a slave and no longer a queen, he could do as he pleased.

"But why? How?" I asked my mother. "He was not special. He wasn't a fire child."

"But he was still a prince."

This time I didn't believe her.

∞

October, 1994. My parents, my younger brother and I are on a bus taking us from New Delhi to Dharamsala, a Himalayan town that also doubles as the capital of the Tibetan Government-In-Exile. We are on a holiday, but for the hundreds of Tibetans who flock to Dharamsala every month, life is too hard to be fun. They come here to pray to the Dalai Lama or to live away from the Chinese occupation of their homeland, preferring the status of "refugee" to the stigma of colonization. Our bus travels on skinny snaking roads that have soaring cliffs on one side and deep valleys on the other. We pass rows and rows of prayer flags, the sets of five colors—blue, white, red, green, yellow—fluttering in the air, representing space, air, fire, water, and earth.

We are the only Hindu-Indian family on the bus, the rest are all Tibetans. They sing, exchange stories, and share homemade foods with each other. They smile at us every now and then, but mostly keep to themselves. At twilight, the bus stops at a roadside dhaaba for bathroom breaks and dinner. We huddle on wooden benches to devour buttery parathas stuffed with mashed potatoes. We drink glass after glass of milky tea spiced with ginger and cardamom that scalds our tongues. The Himalayan wind smacks our faces with icy fingers, but the food in our bellies warms us up as we rush back to the snug cocoon of the bus.

Close to midnight, I am stretched out on my adjustable seat in between sleep and sleeplessness. A butterfly flutters on my neck, its weight flimsy like a shadow. I blink. Surely, I must be dreaming of yellow butterflies beating against a peaceful, blue Himalayan sky. But I am not. The butterfly is a human hand. A man's hand. It's not my brother's. He did not wake me up for a drink of water from the bottle shoved into my backpack. He is fast asleep on the seat next to mine. No, this hand is bigger. It belongs to the Tibetan man sitting behind me.

I turn around in the dark to look at him. I can only see his eyes—shiny beetles, smiling and hungry. I consider waking up my parents. I don't. What if my accusation backfires? What if the four of us are shoved off the bus and left in a crevasse to find our way back to civilization? I yank a lever. I put my seat in an upright position. Now his hand cannot reach me. I tighten the hood of my sweatshirt. I bury myself under my blanket. I spend the night with my back straight as a cliff and only my nose showing. By the time the sun rises outside my window, I am slicked with sweat, my nose frozen to an ice cube.

৪৩

July, 1997. For my seventeenth birthday, my parents decide to buy me a new pair of glasses. They can't be ordinary. They have to be smart. I am headed to college soon. But first, I must get my eyes checked. Our ophthalmologist is someone we have been going to since I was eight. He knows all of us by name. We know he is the same age as my father, his wife is a school teacher, and they have two children.

The morning of the appointment, I tell my parents, "I can go by myself. I don't need a chaperone." They disagree. In their eyes, I am not yet capable enough. I beg. I plead. Finally, they agree.

"Don't mess up," my mother sounds a warning.

I shrug, impatient as I am to get out of the house and escape her overprotective hold. I am almost an adult. I roll my eyes.

Inside his chrome and steel office, the ophthalmologist asks, "Where are your parents?"

I tell him they are home. I add with a laugh that they have finally granted me the permission to travel this short distance on my own and that once he checks my eyesight, I plan on spending an hour at the bookstore next door before returning home.

The ophthalmologist smiles. The sparse hair at his

temples gleams like silver.

He beckons me to sit down, and while looking into my eyes with his many instruments, he reaches out and caresses my face, tucks my errant hair behind my ears, and rubs my shoulders. I purse my mouth and look away.

Once I leave his office, I walk past the bookstore. I return home, my eyes parchment-dry, my secret buried somewhere deep inside.

I don't tell my mother that I have messed up.

৯০

Although the book didn't say so, I always imagined that Draupadi loved peppercorns, little bombs of heat concealed under layers of wrinkled skin. I also imagined that she loved the color indigo and that she wore it everywhere and as often as possible, even on her wedding day, when other Hindu brides typically wear red, gold, maroon, and orange. I want to believe she loved indigo because it brought out the fire of her soot-colored hair.

The year I turn twenty-three, on my way back home from a weekly book bazaar, five men try to rape me on a moving bus. Initially, they give me the impression that aside from the driver and the conductor, the three men are passengers, just like me. But I figure out they are friends when one of them gets up to shut the door, and the conductor leaves his designated seat to sit with them. The bus immediately picks up speed, and they begin to openly discuss their evening plans—all of which involve me, the meat of the day. They call me that. In Hindi and using the crudest words. The meat.

From my point of view, a shattered or dissected leg looks like a small price to pay compared to what they have planned for me. So I jump from the moving bus right to the middle of the road. A car screeches loudly as it slams its brakes and honks, the driver's face a red smear of rage. I don't care. I don't apologize. I run all the way home, saved by a combination of foolishness and daredevilry.

Bit by bit, I tell my parents the entire story. My father sits with his head in his hands. My mother weeps with relief. "You are safe," she says, again and again, like the recurrent bell on an alarm clock.

౫

No one knows for sure how old Draupadi was at the time of her death. While she lived, she birthed five sons, but they were murdered in their sleep in a single night. Each of Draupadi's five husbands took multiple wives. And she made the prophecy come true. She hurt a single man's ego and "caused" the Kurukshetra War, the most terrible carnage Hindu religion and mythology had ever seen. When the War began, each of the warring sides had over a hundred thousand warriors. Eighteen days later, only twelve of them remained.

But she also punished the man who tried to disrobe her inside a crowded assembly. She had his chest ripped open by Bheema, the second of the five brothers, and the husband who loved her the most. She washed her soot-colored hair in the blood that gushed from the wound.

When their final hour approached, the gods instructed Draupadi and her five husbands to climb the

Himalayas. They were on their way to heaven, but because she was the weakest, Draupadi couldn't keep up and fell. None of her husbands stayed back for her. Or with her. They kept walking. Clearly, the threshold to heaven demanded severe sacrifices.

Could it be that Draupadi's husbands were afraid of her? Is that why they abandoned her during their ascent to heaven?

My mother said, "Yes."

This time I believed her.

And I, too, wished I were a fire girl, with indigo clothes and hair the color of soot, instead of an ordinary girl in love with imagination.

Oracles

My aunt, a bureaucrat in India, tells the following story from the time she lead a taskforce against polio. (As of January 2014, India has been declared polio-free by WHO and UNICEF, but a decade ago, the dreaded disease was very much a reality, particularly in the rural parts of the country.) Those days, she would travel with her team through villages under her jurisdiction, dropping off information packets and reminding parents, especially with small children, that vaccinations were available free of cost at all government clinics.

The team often encountered skepticism and curious questions but no open hostility. One afternoon, however, as they waited outside a farmer's house, his heavily-pregnant wife, Sona, rushed out with their three small boys in tow. She ran screaming toward the village lake as if chased by demons and as fast as her bulk would allow.

Alarmed, the team followed Sona. They stood by the shore and watched her wade into the cold water like a mother goose, her children tucked behind her, their teeth chattering, and cheeks dampened by tears.

Sona glared at the government team, particularly at my aunt, their leader. She tightened her grip on the skinny wrists of her children and gathering all the hate she could muster, flung these words in my aunt's direction: "How can you, a woman, be in charge of something this vile? Leave my boys alone, you hear me?" She screeched like a banshee. "I know all about your godless medicine. The oracle has told me about it. You people force it down the throats of boys to make them lose their religion. You turn them impotent. Take one more step in our direction, and I'll drown my boys with my bare hands. I would rather they die than drink your filth."

I laughed when my aunt told me this story. But it was a mirthless laugh; in equal parts sad and horrified. The story was so preposterous, it seemed to belong to a different time, to a different country, a parallel world unrecognizable from the India in which I had been raised. What was especially shocking was that this incident had occurred in West Bengal, a state that prides itself on its seventy percent rate of literacy and whose residents are known to appreciate art, culture, literature, and good cinema.

I assumed Sona belonged to the unfortunate thirty percent of the population that did not have access to education. Perhaps her parents had been so poor they had an "all hands on the deck" policy when she was a child, and they couldn't spare her for a few hours of school every day. Or perhaps they were so conservative and patriarchal, their minds couldn't accept the idea that a girl child needs to be educated. Whatever money they could invest, they did so in her brothers, waiting until she hit puberty so she could be married off to the first man with a square plot of land and a brick home. I lamented over Sona's lack of choices and for her blind and passionate defense of all things religious, since that was clearly the only tool she had ever been given to make sense of the world.

৭৩

I was raised in a secular Hindu home where any religious belief that did not have room for tolerance or inquiry was actively frowned upon. My mother, a staunchly independent thinker, was disdainful toward every discriminatory festival and ritual. She maintained a small shrine inside her bedroom where she offered prayers every morning post her shower. That small ritual was the start and extent of her faith, and she followed no other practices nor required them of her family. My father was openly sarcastic and critical of any religious devotion that he deemed fundamentalist. He wanted his children—my brother and I—to develop inquisitive searching temperaments, so his gifts to us were mostly books and gadgets, like the microscope and telescope.

Although I attended a Catholic school for twelve years of my life, our syllabus wasn't mandated or approved by the Catholic Church. It was state-approved, so we learned the earth was round and life here was the result of the big bang and natural selection. Our teachers, too, came from diverse backgrounds. Most were non-Catholic, married women with children of their own, and there were a handful of male teachers who taught sports and managed the science labs, leaving the nuns in charge of administration.

One day, when I was in the ninth grade, one of our science teachers walked into the classroom dressed like a new bride. Draped in a bright red sari, her face was layered with makeup, and a diamond stud sparkled from her nose. Gold bangles weighed down her wrists, and her hands had clearly been hennaed the night before. What was going on, I wondered. She wasn't a new bride, that much I knew. I overheard some of the girls dissecting her makeup and attire. From snatches of their conversation, two words stood out that explained everything: Karva Chauth, a one-day Hindu festival, mostly celebrated in north India, wherein wives celebrate their husbands and pray for their long lives.

On the appointed day, the dutiful wife wakes up

before sunrise. She bathes, wears rich (if not new) clothes and jewelry, says the right prayers, touches her husband's feet seeking his blessings, eats a ritually sanctioned vegetarian diet devoid of ingredients, such as onion and garlic that Ayurveda cautions are *passion-heightening*, and spends the whole day fasting so the husband can have a long, healthy, and prosperous life. Once the moon rises—given the autumnal time of the year, it rises particularly late—the wife looks at the moon through a sieve, then she looks at her husband through the sieve, and touches his feet again. He feeds her a morsel of food and a sip of water. This breaks the fast, granting her the option to stuff her face with food if she chooses. But the essential idea remains that she must starve and dehydrate herself for a day, and then play peek-a-boo with the moon so her husband may live forever.

At my home, Karva Chauth was not only never celebrated, it was ridiculed. The idea of any of us starving to ensure the long life and health of another was preposterous to my parents and seen as yet another invention of men to keep women down. Which is why when I mentioned my teacher's garb and dedication to the festival, my parents and I laughed. I dismissed her at the dinner table with all the teenage indignation I could muster. "Can you believe this woman is my *science* teacher? She, who thinks the moon—a lifeless, cold, uninhabited satellite of the earth—is a god? Your child's education is basically in the hands of someone blinded by superstition."

I attributed my teacher's nod to Karva Chauth to the strong hold of religion and culture in India. Perhaps she personally dismissed the tradition as silly but couldn't challenge it because most Indian families teach their children, especially girls, how to conform, how to fit in and not stick out in a crowd, and how to follow rituals and cultural habits established for centuries. If only she had been raised in a more accepting climate, I thought sadly. If only she had been taught to think for herself and not bow down to the status quo every step of the way. Surely, such perfect places existed somewhere.

8

When I first arrived in the US, I naïvely believed that the more westward you traveled (by which I mean the western half of the world, not western America per se), the more educated and open-minded you automatically became. I was conditioned by the pictures I saw of the West, particularly of its campuses, where majestic libraries dominated the horizon, and leafy trees cast protective shadows on students as they read, brainstormed over ideas, and assembled elaborate dreams of their future. These worlds seemed magical, thrumming with opportunity. Surely, their citizens would be well-informed. They would be open-minded, tolerant of others, and forever taking advantage of treasures, like free public libraries, the very concept of which seemed unreal in my crowded corner of the globe.

My first job at the University of Idaho was as a teaching assistant to a professor in his religious studies class. There were in all about thirty students, and as expected, the classroom environment was very different from what I had been used to in India. I was impressed by how American students spoke their minds, encouraged as they were by the idea of equality that permeated between the students and the professor. We progressed smoothly from one religion to the next, when one day, the professor decided to go over the commonalities and differences between creation myths from around the world. Among those he used in his discussion were the Judeo-Christian idea of God as an architect; the Maori myth that claims we are all descendants of Rangi and Papa, a common pair of ancestors; and the Boshongo myth from Central Africa where Bumba feels a pain in his stomach, and he vomits out the sun, moon, stars, animals, and humans.

One girl raised her hand, "How can *anyone* believe in the life-producing properties of vomit? Equating these with the Biblical story is stupid. That's the only one that makes sense." Several students nodded. I looked around in surprise. Here we were in 2006, still arguing about the "scientific" validity of the seven-day creation myth.

On an impulse, I asked how many of them actually believed in creationism. Nearly 40% raised their hands. I assumed the professor would come down on them cruelly, like most of mine would have done if I had publicly professed a belief in the Hindu creation myth, where Brahma, the creator, sacrifices himself and from various parts of his body sprout the four castes of Hindus. My classmates would have laughed and never allowed me to forget my lack of rationality. But the American professor did none of that. He cheerfully moved on to the next topic.

That night over dinner, I brought up the topic with my roommate, a graduate student in biology. "How could university students in the most powerful and advanced country of the world think like this?" I asked. I wondered if she had had any similar experiences in her labs. She nodded. After all, when not running extensive experiments, she taught fifty undergraduates the rudiments of science. She told me about the time a student showed up at her office to debate that women have more ribs than men since Eve was forged from one of Adam's. In spite of all the evidence she could present, the student couldn't be convinced that men and women have the same twelve ribs (although in exceptional cases they might have eleven or thirteen).

I tried to understand that young girl's motivation. Here she was, born and raised in America, presumably with easier access to food, water, and shelter than most of the world. She was attending her state's premier university; she had access to scientists and professors, to a massive library that could bring her books from any corner of the globe, and her status as a student gave her the opportunity to peruse and read for free hundreds of print and online journals on science, technology, and medicine. And yet, something in her mind and spirit refused to question the Biblical story of creation. In her stubbornness, she could very well be Sona's sister.

೮

A few months later, a Christian friend invited me to the Sunday service at his church. His pastor was about to deliver a sermon on Islam. I identify myself as a secular Hindu but have always been interested in multi-faith dialogues and have studied contemporary world religions with some degree of seriousness and dedication, so I accepted his invitation immediately. On the appointed day, my friend and I arrived at the church, and I observed the congregation, mostly families with many children, eager to imbibe new insights and learn from the experience.

Learn I did, but it wasn't the kind of education I was expecting. That hour at the church turned out to be the most excruciatingly painful one of my life. The pastor began his sermon with this statement: "Just as we are to sympathize with all those of our brothers and sisters afflicted with cancer, in the same way we are to sympathize with all those afflicted with Islam."

My immediate thought was surely this is the pastor's perverse idea of a joke. I worriedly looked at the congregation, scanning their faces for signs of trouble. I imagined people rising from their seats, some storming out of the hall, others shouting slogans and hurling insults, or perhaps even threatening the pastor and his family with bodily harm to protest the indignity of comparing a deadly disease with the world's second largest faith.

To my immense surprise, nothing of that sort happened. The congregation remained a picture of pastoral tranquility. Row after row of attendees, spanning children to adolescents to adults of every age, listened to the sermon with quiet concentration. Mothers patted snoozing babies, fathers chased after rambunctious toddlers, grandmothers distracted youngsters in their charge with toys and story books, but no one protested.

I could imagine this herd-like atmosphere in a religious gathering in India, all of whose citizens have not yet been guaranteed free and easy access to education, which is why religion often steps in to explain the world. But I couldn't imagine this moment in America, though I was living it. I looked at my friend—educated, erudite, a fellow graduate student at the University of Idaho—completely devoted to the sermon. Afterward, when I told him how disturbed I had been by the pastor's opening statement, he was genuinely surprised that the words, so obviously meant with compassion, had, in fact, offended me.

೫೦

In 2014, a study conducted by the National Science Foundation found that one in four Americans don't know that the Earth orbits the Sun; they believe it to be the other way around. Just like the nearly 50% of the population that believes evolution is a hoax. And yet, perhaps all ignorance isn't necessarily bad, perhaps it can still lead to rewards.

In his book *Ignorance: How It Drives Science*, Dr. Stuart Firestein argues for the coexistence and codependence of science and ignorance. He writes about the time he taught a course titled "Cellular and Molecular Neuroscience" at Columbia University. Almost all of the students were biology majors headed to careers in medicine or research. Their enormous textbook weighed twice as much as the average human brain, and Firestein, like professors everywhere, filled up his lectures with facts in order to sound authoritative. By the end of the semester, however, he felt his lectures were doing a disservice to the students and imparting to them two wrong ideas about science: first, that it was an accumulation of facts, and second, that nearly everything of importance about neuroscience had already been discovered. What was missing from the students' lives was curiosity and wonder, or what Firestein calls, "the exhilaration of the unknown."

So he designed a new course and titled it, "Ignorance: A Science Course." He invited a slew of guest scientists, ranging from astronomers to chemists to statisticians and asked them to talk to students about their own ignorance—what they didn't know in their respective fields, what they wanted to know, the kind of research they would consider valuable and necessary, and the hows and whys of going about it. He hoped that by getting in touch with their ignorance, students would be led to ask better questions, which in turn would lead to better answers.

℣

In my first few years in Idaho, given the miniscule population of Hindus around me, I missed the comings and goings of Karva Chauth. But once I joined Facebook, I stared with disbelief as on the appointed day, my news feed overflowed with updates from giddy girlfriends from back home wishing each other "Happy Karva Chauth" and proudly boasting about their husbands who had sweetly elected to starve themselves in honor of their wives. "What was this national epidemic," I cried? "How was this cute? These were educated, smart women with degrees and jobs. Why were they starving and praying to the freaking moon?" Finally, when I couldn't stand it any longer, I wrote a carefully worded, hopefully inoffensive email and sent it off to several friends. I had to understand their motives. After all, I had grown up with them, and together we had laughed at regressive aspects of our country's religions and cultures. Why this turn around?

My friends not only answered my questions swiftly, but they did so with patience and grace. If they sensed my scorn, they ignored it, allowing me to learn from the diversity of their answers. One said she celebrated the festival because it felt like an Indian and more traditional version of Valentine's Day. Another agreed, adding that she felt pampered the whole day by her husband who showered her with gifts, treated her like a queen, and cooked a sumptuous dinner. A third said she loved dressing up as a bride again and wearing new clothes. A fourth said she appreciated the opportunity it gave her to bond with her mother-in-law and with the women of her extended family and neighborhood, because otherwise, it would be all too easy to miss getting to know them.

Last year, a former classmate invited me to join a WhatsApp group whose fifty or so members were all former classmates and friends. I hadn't been in touch with most of them since 1997, when we graduated from high school. I jumped at the opportunity to reconnect, particularly given my perpetual homesickness. When Karva Chauth rolled in, shyly at first and then encouraged by each other, my friends began posting pictures of themselves—dressed in ritual clothes, flanked by female friends and relatives while on their way to the temple or posing with snacks laid out for after the ceremony.

I scrolled through the pictures and stared at these confident beautiful women, awkward girls no more. Sheathed in vibrant pink and red saris with tasteful jewelry that caught the light in the right places, my classmates weren't oppressed women lacking choices in their lives. These were proud modern women, managing jobs and careers, raising children, taking care of their elderly, and choosing to celebrate a time-honored tradition. They hadn't mutely inherited Karva Chauth from their mothers. They weren't forced to endure it by their mothers-in-law. They had customized it to fit their diverse roles as wives, friends, colleagues, and mothers.

And it seemed fitting that they were sharing these traditional photos via WhatsApp, a nod to Indians' love for both the past and the future.

Perhaps all those years ago, my science teacher had also done the same. She had taught us about DNA and evolution and exercised her personal choice with respect to the ancient festival she wanted to celebrate. But by making my tunnel vision my only oracle, I had missed it.

ॐ

It is January 2015, a decade since I first heard Sona's story. I call my aunt to tell her I am writing an essay on science and superstition and the peculiar ways in which they exist in India and America. I ask her if she remembers Sona and when she says "yes," I tell her parallel stories from America. I hear the incredulity in her voice. She echoes what I once believed to be true: the more westward you travel, the more enlightened you become. She wonders out loud if ignorance, especially in prosperous countries, is really a matter of choice.

I hesitate, unsure of how to answer. Perhaps ignorance is really the same everywhere, a combination of patriarchy and conservatism, of parents passing along their fear of everything that is alien or different to their children, of the need to belong and fit in with friends or family in a fiercely independent-minded society like America, where getting a driver's license as a teenager is as much of a rite of passage as the sacred thread ceremony was a hundred years ago for Brahmin boys in India.

I tell my aunt the many ways in which coming westward has made me less ignorant. It has given me access to more varieties of people and beliefs, introduced me to new foods, and made me more politically correct. It has taught me to watch for things I once didn't, such as my carbon footprint. I now have a definite idea how small I want to live, for in the end, I can only account for myself.

I try to dispel ignorance in my own limited way inside my classroom. So what if I am not leading my students toward cutting-edge scientific experiments, and instead, they are writing essays on their childhood or their first kitchens? I assign essays, such as Jonathan Stern's *The Lonely Planet Guide to My Apartment,* Binyavanga Wainaina's *How to Write About Africa* and Marie Nasta's *On Being a Mistress*—essays that are brilliant, astonishing, and timeless. I watch my students' faces fill with surprise, shock even, at the ways in which these writers have taken predictable topics and turned them upside down on their heads and subverted the norm.

One of my favorite writing exercises is when I instruct my students to leave the classroom and walk around for ten minutes, counting the number of times their favorite color appears in their surroundings. They count it on people's clothes, bags, shoes, on paintings and posters along the wall, and they return to their seats, surprised that in spite of having walked down that same corridor for months and sometimes years, they had missed so many obvious details.

I brim with pride at their discovery, at their "exhilaration of the unknown," although this color-writing exercise is a small thing that will neither change the world nor transform my students into inquisitive, well-informed citizens of the world. But it is their willingness to look at these old details through new insight that I laud. That gives me hope. Perhaps, one of Sona's sons, too, is helping her look past the oracle at the world anew.

Five Students

1: Nick

On the first day of class, you said *Tom Sawyer* was your favorite book. When I asked why, you shrugged. "It's a boy's book through and through. Tom and I aren't from the same worlds, but we are pretty similar." I noticed the way your female classmates looked at you. "Too pretty," I thought. "Life has probably been kinder to you than it has to most others."

As the semester progressed, you surprised me with your commitment to the readings and by the number of times you stayed after class to discuss upcoming assignments. I liked the energy with which you assembled a writing group. Thanks to the essays you wrote and so readily shared in class, I thought I sort of knew you. You loved chocolate chip cookies. You worked at a nearby gas station. Once, I ran into you and your sister, and you introduced her with pride.

And then you sent me that email. When I clicked it open, I saw it contained an attachment, which surprised me because no assignments were due. Your email contained only one line, "This is the story I want to write but I can't." I opened the attachment.

It was short. Devastation in 300 words. About the time you got drunk at a bar and didn't want to drive. A man you met there offered to drop you home. He held your arm as you staggered up the stairs. He eased you into your bed. And then he unbuttoned your jeans, yanked them off. You foamed protests. Then you passed out. You don't remember much else of what happened that night. In the morning, you pretended all you suffered from was a hangover. You kept running into him in our small town. Neither of you ever talked about what happened.

I sat unblinking at my screen. I wrote back immediately. I begged you to report the crime. You refused. Was it an honor code thing? Something that makes it that much harder for men to talk about such vulnerabilities?

Inside the classroom the next day, I paced while all of you furiously scratched out a quick, ten-minute essay in your journals. I noticed for the first time that our classroom didn't have any windows, a detail that may have pleased me in the past. One less source of distraction. But that day I plucked at my collar, as the room breathed down my neck. It was a beautiful spring day, a miracle worth noting given the bleak pummeling all of us in north Idaho had received that winter.

I picked up the syllabus and silently read my disclaimer: "The contents of this syllabus may alter at the instructor's discretion." I reread the word "discretion." *The freedom to decide what should be done in a particular situation.* I thought of grace and forgiveness.

2: Jessica

On the first day of class, your introduction was interspersed with many a nervous giggle. You told your classmates and me that you were here in Idaho from Arizona, and that you knew little to nothing about the world outside. The confession was meant to be cute and self-effacing. I was unimpressed, although I hid it under my stock, welcome-to-college smile. I took in your gleaming hair and skinny white jeans and dismissed you as one of the many giggly freshmen dispersed across campus, far more invested in the deliberate messiness of your chic clothes than perhaps the messy, third-world conditions in which they were sewn.

The following week, with casual nonchalance, as if we were two acquaintances discussing the merits of a new restaurant, you told me about the neurological disorder you have had since birth. Laughing, you warned me there was a chance you could have a seizure inside the classroom, and in that case, I was not to panic but leave you alone until it subsided.

Fortunately, it never came to that. The semester went smoothly and pulled to a close without pausing even for a hiccup. For a girl who confessed to not knowing anything about the world, you participated in every discussion with passion and ferocity.

In your last email of the semester, you wrote:

Dear Professor Dasgupta, before your class, I didn't think Hinduism was even an actual religion. I believed it to be a cult, something to do with Buddha. I didn't know Muhammad was to Islam what Christ was to Christianity. I thought Mohammad was just a dude, like maybe from the Bible, who hung out with Jesus. I wasn't quite sure what an Arab was. I have recently made friends with a boy from Quwate (sic) and I feel I will learn a lot from him. Thank you for all that you have taught me.

I don't usually save old emails but yours I have. I return to it often. It's my talisman, a good reminder of why I do what I do, why I love my job, why it's important to have this job. And why my cynicism must often be issued a warning.

3: Abdul

On the first day of your freshman class on world religions, you introduced yourself to us with a fine lilting accent. Your classmates, mostly Idahoans, mostly eighteen-year-olds, looked at you with interest. They took in your thick dark hair, your neatly trimmed mustache, and your expansive hand gestures. For many of them, you were the first Arab they had ever encountered. When you mentioned your country, there were a few uncertain glances, the question "Is that in the Middle East?" writ large upon confused faces.

As the semester unfolded, I discovered you were mostly quiet inside the classroom, the relative unfamiliarity with English clunky on your body like armor. But what you lacked in vocabulary you more than made up with your smile and enthusiasm. Outside the classroom, I ran into you several times—at the food court, inside the library, in line to get coffee. You were always surrounded by friends from home, and you seemed a different person—loud, boisterous, cocooned, and comforted by Arabic.

We wrapped up the unit on Hinduism a day before Diwali, the biggest Hindu festival, and I confessed to you and your classmates that I was homesick for New Delhi. I could imagine the streets lit up, the shops and homes aglow with candles and earthen lamps, the neighbors setting off continuous streams of fireworks, and my parents busy welcoming visitors bearing gift boxes wrapped in silk and stuffed with dates, cashews, sweets, and chocolates.

Spontaneously, you all voted for a class party. I gave in, not that I needed much persuading. On the appointed day, everyone showed up with their contributions: cookies, pretzels, chips and salsa, Pepsi and Coke. I brought in the coconut laddoos I had made the previous night using an abbreviated version of my grandmother's recipe: first, toast the unsweetened coconut flakes, then add a can of condensed milk, slivered almonds, chopped raisins, and freshly ground cardamom. Roll the cooled mixture into little balls of nutty goodness. Cover with parchment paper.

On the day of the party, you knocked on our classroom door twenty minutes late. My first impulse was to shoo you off for being tardy. But instead, two other students had to hold the doors open so you could lug in the enormous steel cauldron you and your friend carried from each side. You set it up on my desk and lifted its lid. Beaming, you announced, "Chicken *machboos.*"

Our classroom, bland from the fluorescent white lights and white walls, misted up with the scent of cinnamon and garlic, saffron and cloves. You had cooked enough drumsticks to feed your classmates three times over. But before any of them could pounce on the chicken, you filled up a plate and brought it to me. "First, I serve the teacher as per my custom and faith," you explained shyly. Your classmates understood and respectfully awaited their turn.

A week later, we began the unit on Islam. Like every other year, I asked everyone to tell me what comes to their minds when they hear the terms "Islam" and "Muslim." You watched with mild amusement as your classmates rattled off the predictable: "Middle East," "Arabs," and "Saudis." But you folded in on yourself, your smile gradually disappearing as they also spewed out "terrorism," "radicalism," "hatred," in the same breath as the inexplicable "curly hair," "mud huts," and "flying carpets."

Your smile, however, returned when a boy the same age as you, but from a family in southern Idaho that I imagine to be very different from yours, confessed he had never met a Muslim prior to you and had, in fact, always been wary. But since our Diwali party, his idea of Islam was your delicious food and generosity.

It was a bittersweet moment, wasn't it? On the one hand, your hospitality had cut through at least one person's previously held notion of what it means to be a Muslim. On the other, it was a sharp reminder that even though that's all it takes—a few weeks of interaction, one shared meal—most of us will never pause long enough to rearrange our prejudices and take that first bite.

4: John

On the first day of class, you sat on the very last seat. You didn't say much. You quietly observed, and I assumed you were one of those shy quiet types. How wrong I was. Within a week, I learned that you were feisty and passionate, opinionated but respectful. Your faith in Christianity and keen interest in other religions didn't stem from sentimentality or from the because-my-parents-told-me-so textbook. It was grounded in a close study of texts.

The day you submitted your first essay, you met me after class and asked, "Could I submit a revised copy?"

I must have looked confused. "Revised copy of what? I haven't even started grading yet. What are you going to revise?"

You shrugged. "Just what I turned in. Our class discussion made me realize that I need to add about five more points."

A few weeks later, you asked if we could carry on debating after class. Over coffee. I agreed. My own college professors had generously mentored me in their free time. It was only fair that I continue the tradition. And so we began to meet, once every few weeks, over coffee, to debate, discuss, and argue. You asked how it was possible for me to live so far away from home in Idaho. You said you were toying with the idea of doing something new and unfamiliar. Was there a technique for success? A foolproof plan?

Here's what I told you—give the new city or town or hamlet ninety days. And make five friends. Five good people. That is all.

You invited me to see a documentary. You had directed it yourself. Its purpose was to shed light on urban poverty. You had traveled across five states for research and interviews. On the appointed evening, I arrived at the indie theater downtown, expecting to see a handful of your friends and beaming members of your family. How wrong I was.

The theater was packed. The town couldn't be more proud.

The documentary was layered with Christian themes, but even the nonbeliever in me was touched by the humanity of your work. There was no mistaking your talent. Or the singularity of your focus. Or did my pride as your teacher fog up my critical lens?

The following semester, you asked me for a recommendation letter. I said, *Yes, of course*. I assumed you were headed to film school. How wrong I was. Your destination was a monastery.

You don't want a recommendation letter from me, I protested. *It will ruin your chances. We play for two very different teams.* You dismissed my fears. *Just tell them how much we argue.*

I did. I wrote a good letter, one with fighting chances. But I fought even harder to keep you in school. Finish graduation. Pack you off to study films. But you never had any doubts. Your mind was made up. The afternoon you left, I fought off tears, but your stubborn dedication filled me with pride.

A week later, I received a check in the mail for forty dollars. The accompanying note read, "The last of my money for your coffee. It might not be enough for ninety days, but you should still be able to meet five friends."

5: Mitch

On the first day of class, you wore glasses and a hesitant smile. In the following weeks, you showed up well-prepared and ready with questions, eager to learn. And then one day, you disappeared—from the classroom, the roster, and the university.

Barely a week later, you sent me a friend request on Facebook. But here, too, your appearance was sporadic. A few months later, when your profile picture popped up again on my news feed, you weren't alone. You were posing with a raven-haired girl with a clotted-cream complexion. Your long skinny arms were draped around her pregnant stomach. I checked your ages. You were both nineteen, one wobbly month apart from each other, teenagers playing dress-up. Your floppy hair covered your forehead. Your chin was an acne playground. Your "About Me" section announced that you're now a sales executive at a video store. Are video stores going to be around for long?

I Wikipedia-ed the tiny Alaskan town you identified as your hometown. I learned that its population is 3000 and that it has five playgrounds, six churches, three radio stations, and one newspaper. Five years before you were born, there was an oil spill, one of the most devastating in the history of America. It wiped out entire schools of salmon and herring, your town's primary source of livelihood. The most notable person is a hundred years old, and her claim to fame is her ability to speak her tribe's native language.

It was college that brought you to Idaho. But you no longer lived in our university town. You had moved someplace else. I looked it up, your new hometown, where you shared your life with your pregnant girlfriend. Its population is less than 2000. According to Wikipedia, your town does not have a single notable person.

Your girlfriend's high school diploma is from an online school with the word "freedom" followed by an exclamation mark in its motto. Her favorite movie is *Titanic*. I cannot help but notice the poor spellings, the lack of punctuation and apostrophes. All her posts are about your generosity, your gifts of coffee, chocolates, and a bracelet. Every picture is a selfie and there are over 300 of them, angled to show off her pretty eyes and her constantly changing hair color—red, yellow, dark brown, black with highlights. She wants to get rid of her five-month-old puppy. She only wants $100 for it.

I read one of your poems. The one about the beauty of the sun and spring, of running one's hands through blades of grass. And I wonder what I could have said to keep you in school.

Beyond the Ivory Tower

It was a friendly phone call that informed me that I had won first prize in the Latah County Fair's Lucky Draw and that it was waiting to be picked up at the Moscow Public Library. The news was an exciting addition to the eye-opening fair, packed with many firsts: my first taste of doughy-sugary-fried-goodness elephant ears; the first time I touched a cow, a horse, and a sow; and my first insight into a world where quilting grandmothers sauntered like Hollywood royalty.

At the library the next day, a woman with hair the color of coffee sat at the front desk. A cluster of toddlers hovered around an aquarium. Two elderly women studied the spines of books whose shelves read, "Large Print."

When I explained the purpose of my visit and offered to show her my ID, the front desk lady laughed. "Hon," she said, "if you can spell your name, that's proof enough for me."

I did. S-A-Y-A-N-T-A-N-I.

She pressed into my hands a gleaming basket. The cellophane-wrapped goodies included books, a scented candle, packets of microwaveable popcorn, a clutch of bookmarks and paperweights, and the kind of reading light you can affix to your page. I, the broke graduate student, hugged the basket. So this is how it felt to win the code to Aladdin's treasure-filled cave.

If it hadn't been for the prize, I don't know when I would have discovered the public library. After all, I had access to the university's vastly superior collections, where I had only to pick a subject and if the relevant book(s) weren't available on the shelves, they were made so— perched on the wings of modern technology, they flew in from archives practically anywhere in the world.

Shortly thereafter, I became a member of the

public library, pulled in by the sight of the people I had glimpsed on my first visit. They piqued my curiosity. How did those outside the university live? How identical were they to the Americana I had absorbed from books and television all those years when I had viewed it from outside? Everyone I knew, everyone I was friends with, was a direct result of my association with the university. They were colleagues, classmates, teachers, or former students. The university never left me; I carried it within myself, even when I stepped out to grab a beer or a cup of coffee.

I grew up in a family in love with books and reading, but libraries didn't feature prominently in my childhood. There just weren't enough of them to serve us all in the sheer enormity that is New Delhi.

My school library was the size of a large living room. The first time we were led in there as a class was in sixth grade. The room seemed cavernous. It gleamed with dark wood furniture and inside the glass cases, the books shone like promises. I don't know about my classmates, but I felt tall, a grown up. I want to think I hid my nervousness well. Our librarian was a kind and matronly lady, and over the years as I became a frequent visitor, she let me borrow more books than the school-issued library card allowed, and more often than not, she pointed me toward "adult" books she thought I could handle.

The lending library I most frequented as a teenager was a short bike ride away from home. It was a table on a sidewalk, covered with tarpaulin, with the owner on a wobbly chair behind it. Next to him on a low stool was a cashbox made of grey metal. I assume he had to pay the local police constable a regular and hefty fee for the privilege of occupying the sidewalk. He charged five rupees per book. I would bike down after school, pick up a book or two, devour them overnight, and return the next evening. With my limited pocket money, this quickly became an expensive hobby. I don't know whether it was out of pity or because it made financial sense to hold on to a loyal customer, he often let me borrow two books for the price of one. He was big, mustachioed, with an oily face and slicked-back hair. He wore striped shirts over tight pants and in an alternate reality, he could very easily have subbed for any of the villain parts in the Hindi movies of my childhood. But he didn't. He himself spoke only in Hindi but by stocking all the series I loved, he strengthened my love for the English language.

I still remember that gesture with gratitude. I was a thirteen-year-old by then. I wasn't doing favorably at school. I was bored in most of my classes and frustrated by teachers who were strict disciplinarians, who canceled periods like art and library at their whim to fit in extra hours of classwork. There was no fighting their clear message of what we should consider priorities and what we should discard. I felt like a misfit in our neighborhood as well. We had moved to this location just a year ago, from the home barely two kilometers away, where I had spent my childhood and left behind familiar faces. We were still in the same zip code and the new neighborhood signaled my parents' increasing prosperity, but it also leached into my life the competitiveness, anxiety, and insecurities inherent among teenagers everywhere.

But the man with the table-for-a-lending-library was one of my anchors. I am thankful for the freedom I had to negotiate with him on my own, armed with only my bicycle and limited allowance and without my parents hovering over my shoulder. I don't know if present-day kids have that luxury, surrounded as they are by overprotective parents and schools, shielded from the world by smartphones and noisy apps.

೮

The perimeters of Moscow Public Library's two-story, grey-stone building are marked by crabapple trees. The bright red fruits that can pass for mini Roma tomatoes hang in cheerful uneven clumps. Inside, the low ceiling makes me feel small but safe. The walls smell of newsprint, old and young books, fresh flowers, and someone's covert cup of coffee and sandwiches. The posters inform about events within the larger community and signs that remind everyone to silence their cell phones out of respect for others. Between 10 a.m. and 6 p.m. six days a week, the library thrums with the staccato click of keyboards, the whirr of the air conditioner, the pulling out and pushing back of books, the sifting of pages, the hushed crunch of nuts, and the thump of heavy backpacks as they settle on the floor. Librarians talk to patrons. Book club members swap notes and meeting dates. Writing groups decide whose stories they should workshop next. Neighbors, with aisles between them instead of fences, exchange notes on when to plant tulips. On Saturdays, children run down the carpeted hall toward their section. The toddlers stare and point at the aquarium. They tap on the glass, hold elaborate conversations with the fish. Clearly, silence cannot be expected from every patron.

Here, there aren't mile-long shelves of encyclopedias, no mammoth piles of dictionaries and thesauruses, no floor-after-floor of space dedicated to books on subjects ranging from the mating habits of the tsetse fly to the creation of African identity in Meso-America. But here, there are magazines on quilting and beading, on remodeling barns and antique furniture, and recipe books that can teach you how to cook for four on less than ten dollars. The romance novels wear red-heart stickers on their spines and promise to reveal all about *When Harry Met Molly, The Christmas Wedding Ring,* and *The Taste of Innocence,* while the Westerns flaunt titles, such as *Summer of the Gun, Apache Canyon,* and *Sin Killer.*

    I share my table with ladies who exchange crock-pot recipes, with junior high students squirming under the hawk-eyes of their tutors, with young women in long skirts and thick braids writing pen and paper old-fashioned letters, and with mentors and mentees hashing out the finer points of foreign languages. I see couples looking up employment opportunities, counting food stamps, and cataloging coupons. I make way for large families tumbling in with children ranging from the just-born to adolescence, their parents struggling to reign them in and not scatter like rolling pins. I have become familiar—in the way you become familiar with the same people you see every day at the bus stop—with the elderly gentleman who wears a hat and oversize blue jeans and comes in every afternoon and occupies the same chair in the travel section. He picks up a book, flips it open to a random page and starts to read. Within minutes, he falls asleep, his beard tucked in between the top two buttons of his shirt. I imagine he dreads the clock the most as it makes its way toward the closing hour, indicating in no uncertain terms that it's time for all of us to go home.

Once, on my way to the water fountain, I had to walk past an acne-marked teenager watching something with great intent on one of the desktop computers set up for public use. There was something awkward about his slouch. I paused. He was checking out porn. Even the back of his head was smiling.

At the public library, I people watch as much as I read. I eavesdrop shamelessly. I confess my vice to my writing students. I tell them to hone their listening skills because it will make them better writers, because it will give them valuable insight into how real people talk, and what their body language suggests even though their words might be saying something entirely different. I don't tell them to eavesdrop because it's a quick fix for loneliness or because it is an ode to a time when you could still belong somewhere without logging into Facebook or chasing celebrities on Twitter.

It shocks them, this blatant disregard for other people's privacy, but they do it, often with surprising results. They come back to the class shaking their heads, declaring in loud voices all that they have now learned not to disclose in public and admitting that the inspiration to write can lie in a kernel of the most banal conversation.

∞

In his essay, "Let Us Now Praise Libraries," Anthony Doerr writes, "...good librarians [are] like drug dealers." He extorts them to "keep pushing the product... because as every good dealer knows, all it takes is one fix and your patrons are hooked."

I think librarians are more like superheroes, especially in a community library. Here, they are shamans and faith healers. They are warriors. Custodians. They whisper soothing words to tired toddlers unwilling to stand in line. They teach how to get on "the goddamn internet" to the generation that must now learn to pay utility bills online. They help settle the nervous spouses of international scholars and visitors, who have fearlessly followed them to America in their quests for jobs and degrees but are afraid of their little grasp over English.

I wish such community libraries existed back in my childhood in New Delhi. How thrilling would it have been to check out, rightfully, numerous books at the same time. To have known that individuals and institutions exist to ferry books out of neighboring towns just for me. To have authors visible and available for readings and to participate in community activities, such as read-alongs, story times, design-your-own-bookmarks. What would I have done with all that luxury and privilege? That unique entitlement?

I know I romanticize libraries. I believe they possess gravitas. Because that's what books do. They grant gravitas, dignity, to our otherwise ordinary lives. But in the case of the Moscow Public Library and others of its kind, their gravitas is not the value which keeps bringing me back. It's the changing luminous forms of those that stand in between the aisles, the adventures they imagine when they pick up *Eat, Pray, Love*, when they fall asleep with their face pasted to *Reader's Digest*, when they surreptitiously open a smuggled-in candy bar.

The Butcher Shop of New Delhi

That Sunday morning I was excited by the prospect of the dinner party my parents were hosting later in the day. I was six years old, an only child, and the birth of my brother was still two years away. My parents were young and so were their friends. I addressed them as aunts and uncles even though we were not biologically related. Often, at their parties and such, I either ended up as the only kid or the only kid my age. Others were far too young, still in the grasps of their mothers. But I didn't mind. Most of my parents' friends treated me like a real person. They didn't baby me, and I felt welcome and comfortable in the world of adults.

On that Sunday, too, like all other times we had hosted parties, it was a given that Baba would run errands and buy groceries, and Ma would tidy things up at home, prep and cook the feast. It was a blistery morning, and the air tasted of dust, and yet, I didn't opt to stay inside the cool rooms of our apartment. I accompanied Baba instead. There were two reasons for it: first, the possibility that we would stop at our local bookstore, and I would be allowed to pick up a new book of my choice. Additionally, if I behaved really well, there was the chance reward of a lemon popsicle. And the fruity iciness combined with a newly-purchased book would equal perfection, paradise, and pure happiness in that oppressive New Delhi heat.

We stepped out after breakfast and for the next couple of hours, Baba and I zipped in and out of chaotic streets on his pistachio scooter, my arms cinched around his waist, and my face pressed against his back. It wasn't long before I began to lose count of all the fresh fruits and vegetables we had bought. With each new destination, my energy levels plummeted. The sun shone so bright, it hurt my eyes. My throat felt like stone. I longed to return home so I could lie down on the cool mosaic floor of the drawing room with a book. I could already picture Ma hovering in the background with a tall glass of lemonade, coaxing me to freshen up so we could all eat lunch together. At every stop, I tugged at the thin shoulder straps to air out my dress. When we had left home, the white cotton with blue flowers had felt like air and smelled of soap. Now, pasted to my skin, it stank of exhaustion.

Our last stop was the butcher shop. Though it was air-conditioned, a detail that didn't escape me because the blast of cold air was something to look forward to, the butcher himself always had layers of perspiration glazing his forehead. Sure, cutting meat was a physical enough activity, but somehow it didn't seem deserving of all that sweat.

The butcher was a fierce-looking, heavy-set Muslim man. He wore grey cotton kurtas that were always too tight. His thick glossy mustache matched his oil-slicked, parted-in-the middle hair. His lips were black from the tobacco he kept wadded in his mouth. Worse, he never smiled. Every time a customer walked in, he gave a curt nod as he listened to the order, then bellowed instructions, and returned to dismembering bones and joints with a cleaver that made a distinct *thwok thwok thwok* noise.

The butcher and his two assistants sat on a marble platform that started near the entrance and ran the entire length of the shop, all the way to the back. Their tools rested on enormous blocks of wood—tree stumps really—stained rust and ruby from all the blood and juices they had absorbed over the years. The blocks were positioned in front of them like desks. Some of the knives resembled swords and scimitars, their pointy ends curved like the letter C. Others had blades flat as bricks and looked unwieldy to maneuver. Those reminded me of hammers; I had seen them decimate big slabs of meat into granules.

And then there were the carcasses. They hung from tall iron hooks embedded deep into the ceiling. Once they had been flesh and blood animals—lambs— but now stripped of skin and hair, they were nothing more than bone and muscle. Combined with the scent of soap, they gave the butcher shop its own peculiar smell.

Most days, I found the ritual of cutting and carving meat fascinating. I would watch the glint of the knife as it swooped down to make a precise incision, the dull thud of cleaver against bone where meat met steel, becoming rectangles of lamb that were wrapped in plastic and handed to my father, which Ma magically turned into her peppery lamb curry.

But that Sunday afternoon, I was whiney and needy, the way I suppose six-year-olds can be, and now when I look back, I see my father's dilemma. Should he have dropped me off at home and returned by himself to the butcher shop? But the lamb needed time to cook. Should he have dropped me off at a friend's home instead? But who would have enjoyed the intrusion of a cranky kid on a Sunday afternoon? The bookstore would have been an excellent option, except it was in a different neighborhood and probably already shuttered down for the owner's post-lunch nap.

In the midst of this dilemma, the sight of that new toy store must have given my father hope. It must have shimmered like an oasis across the street from the butcher shop. Or maybe it wasn't Baba who spotted it first. Maybe I did. Or we both did, together. At the same time. That detail doesn't matter anymore. What matters is our instinctive immediate relief at having found a solution to our problem.

I see it all now: Baba holds me by my hand and leads me to the store. Inside, it's so pleasantly cool that I feel as if I am walking through ice cream. It is incredible to be out of the sun for however short a while. My eyes devour the treasures—boxes of mechanized toys and cars, wicker baskets full of stuffed animals, glass cases displaying an immense variety of dolls, elaborate kitchen and bathroom sets perfect for playing house, and the glistening spines of hundreds of shiny new books.

An old man steps out from behind a candy-stocked counter. "Hello," he says, smiling, "Looking for something specific?"

The man is taller than Baba, but his hair is white. He reminds me of someone's grandfather. When he smiles, his eyes crinkle. Even though he is facing Baba, he turns ever so slightly to include me in the conversation. I like that. I let go of Baba's hand.

Baba says, "I was wondering if I could leave my daughter here for ten minutes? I have to run to the butcher shop," he points with his shoulder in its direction, "and she is exhausted."

"Of course, of course, take your time," the man smiles. "We will be fine, won't we?"

I give him a shy nod, delighted that I will have full run of this wonderland, without the disciplining presence of my father.

Baba says, "Be good, okay?"

I nod, barely able to contain my excitement. I am no longer hungry nor thirsty nor tired. I cannot wait for Baba to leave.

But as soon as he does, I am stumped by all the

choices. I don't know which way to turn—there is a colorful wicker basket spilling with stuffed bears, bunnies, and pandas. I notice beautiful bookshelves lined with titles I have never seen before, and dolls, those pudgy ones that look like babies or the lean, lady-like ones. I wonder if I should touch them or grab them all in my arms.

And what's more, this man even has Barbies—rows and rows of them that are shimmering at me. They look elegant, beautiful, and expensive. Only a handful of my friends have Barbies. I inch closer to the shelf and gaze with adoration at the one closest to me. She is sheathed in a pink silk gown with a slight dusting of silver stars. Her elaborately styled hair is the color of gold.

I ache to hold her. I want to touch her dress. I want to feel the luxurious thickness of her gold hair between my fingers. But I know I can't. I mustn't. Because Barbie is in her telltale pink box. I am only supposed to look and not touch. Because if the box breaks, Baba will have to buy it. And somehow today just doesn't seem like it will be a doll-buying kind of day.

"Do you want to see her properly?"

I spin around, surprised. The man has come around the corner and is now standing next to me. Well, this *is* his store. He can stand wherever he wants. I shake my head, unable to trust my voice. I want to say "Yes" but I don't. I can hear Baba's cautionary words.

"Come on," the man insists, "I can tell you want to see Barbie properly. What do you think? Shall we take her out? Shall we play with her for a while?" The man's words are better than a lemon popsicle.

I swallow hard. I shake my head again. "I am not supposed to touch because then Baba will have to buy me the Barbie," I explain. My eyes remain glued to the pink box.

The man laughs. "Don't worry. We won't tell him. You and I will just play with Barbie for a little while. This will be our secret."

I nod even though it is a strange suggestion. No adult male, neither my father nor any of my uncles, has ever offered to play with dolls. Every evening when Baba returns from work, he and I play variations of hide and seek. With my uncles, I usually play Teacher-Teacher, where I pretend to be Miss Bawa, my own stern teacher in school, and they, my dutiful students. This man's offer to play with dolls is new. Unfamiliar.

I look up to see if he is joking. "May I really play with Barbie?"

"Yes," he says, "Really." He pulls out Barbie's tall pink box from the shelf. Gently, as if she is a real person, he eases her out and puts her into my hands. I touch her hair, almost with reverence. It's just as I had imagined: a luminous cloud, a silk scarf. Her dress glows, the stars glitter between my fingers. Her face, however, is cold and plastic-y, just like my other dolls.

The grandfatherly man brings out a chair from somewhere and sets it down. He lifts me up and puts me on his lap. I am a little surprised but not alarmed by this rush of affection. I still have clear memories of adults putting me on their laps and reading to me. I make myself comfortable. From my spot, I can see a sliver of the main entrance. The man, given his height, must have been able to see more—anyone heading toward his store or exiting the ones across the street. Like the butcher shop.

Wordlessly, he pulls Barbie out of my hands. I blink. What have I done wrong? I glance at the main entrance. Is Baba already back? Is he hurriedly stowing

Barbie away so Baba won't find out? The man starts to hum and with a deft stroke, pulls Barbie's dress to the top of her head. I cannot see her smiling face any more. Instead, I see her white panties and the underside of her dress. It's rough and ugly like a sack, so different from the silky starry top.

The man extends a finger and strokes Barbie's chest, which is not flat like mine. She has breasts like grownup girls. I alternate between staring at Barbie and the man's face. He can play with Barbie whenever he wants. Why does he have to encroach on my limited time?

He rests his bony finger on Barbie's chest and asks, "Do you have these?" I shake my head. He puts a hand on my chest as if to check and rubs the whole area, slowly but carefully. His finger now slides down to Barbie's white panties. He rubs it. Back and forth. Back. And. Forth. Slowly, lovingly, deliberately. "Are you also wearing white panties like her?" he asks.

I shake my head again. I don't have white panties. Not even one.

"No?" he smiles and licks his lips, "Let's check, shall we?"

He places Barbie on the floor and tugs at my cotton dress. I am not sure what game this is, but I don't want to play it anymore. I protest, "Only Ma can see my panties."

The man's grip is firm. "Don't worry," he assures me, "we will have fun, you will see."

He pulls up my dress and stares. He runs his tongue over his teeth. He scoops Barbie up from the floor but keeps her face covered by her bundled-up dress. He slides his finger under her panties. It's an ugly awkward swelling, like a tiny ghost draped in a white sheet. Then his finger starts to move and twitch, as if it's shy, as if it doesn't want to come out. It just wants to stay in and play this odd game of hide-and-seek.

"Isn't this fun?" the man asks. His voice sounds strange. "You know what will be more fun? If we do this to you."

I try to get off his lap, but with his free arm he pins me to himself. "No."

He tugs at my frock again, and I repeat, more loudly, "No. Only Ma can see this."

"Come on. Don't be a spoilsport. We have to keep playing."

There is a snap of my panties' elastic, and suddenly I can feel his fingers. It's an odd sensation, one that I've never experienced before. I feel the scrape of his nails as he rubs and prods me in unfamiliar places.

The game stops just as abruptly as it started. He hurriedly straightens my dress, sets me down on the floor and glides Barbie back into her pink plastic home. Almost immediately, Baba walks into the store, his fingers threaded through two plastic bags.

I run to him.

Baba says, "You know what? The butcher asked about you today. 'Where is your little girl?' I told him you were here. He said, 'Hello.'"

The toy-store owner has returned to his spot behind the counter. He appears to be busy arranging and rearranging boxes.

"Did you like any of the books?" Baba asks.

"I don't want any. I want to go home."

I can tell Baba is relieved. He waves to the man, "Thanks for letting her wait here."

"No problem. She is a good little girl. Please

stop by again."

I grip Baba's hand, "I want to go home."

"Yes, let's," Baba says, putting on his sunglasses. "Even I am tired. Well, at least Ma will be pleased. Today's meat is tender and fresh."

৪১

The rest of that Sunday is a blur in my mind. I think once Baba and I reached home, the sheer relief of being with Ma inside our cool apartment and under the reassuring whirr of the bedroom ceiling fan, put me to a dreamless nap. When I awoke, the excitement of the evening overshadowed the memory of everything else that had occurred earlier that day.

And that's how it remained for years and years, the memory dormant and quiet, unwilling to stir or create a scene. I accompanied my father to the butcher shop numerous times, but never again did I step inside the toy store. From time to time, I would remember the incident—what had happened in front of those pink Barbies and glass cases, but I rejected it, or tried to, believing it hadn't done me any permanent damage.

Until twenty years later, one weekend in Idaho, when I set out with two girlfriends for a writing retreat in the mountains just a couple of hours north of Moscow. It was a picturesque drive, with nothing to interrupt us except the purr of the car's engine and our excited chatter, thrilled as we were for the opportunity to get away from the rigors of grad school and into a world with no internet and only limited cellphone coverage. Somewhere along the drive, the conversation turned to monsters, and suddenly each of us, though separated by geography, race, and nationality, had something to share.

My voice shook as the toy-store owner took over the car. Up to that moment, I had never talked about him, not to my parents, nor to my close friends. I had convinced myself that it was a small incident, one that should not be paid any attention, especially given that searing unfathomable tragedies occur every second in India. Surely, no one should have to expend their time and energy on a small story from over twenty years ago. Surely, the incident could not have left a scar.

But it had. And I had needed Idaho, the distance from India, and my friends' outrage to understand it and to realize that even in developed countries such as America, monsters exist, and that here, too, they get away because their victims experience the same agonizing trap of shame, loathing, and embarrassment.

When we reached the cabin, I set aside my laptop. I no longer wanted to write what I had planned for the weekend. Our conversation had ignited something and lent the story an urgency. It needed a physical release, not the sterile click-clack of typing on the keyboard, but the violence of pen against paper. I wrote feverishly. Messily. I recounted every detail of the day. But I couldn't remember the specifics of the man's face. What kind of a nose did he have? What color were his eyes? Did he wear glasses? I wrote everything else from the abrasive heat of the city to how the man's fingers had felt against my skin. But I couldn't remember if he wore rings or bracelets or a watch. If he had a cap. Or bad teeth. He did have white hair though, didn't he? Or was that also my imagination? Why was my memory so unreliable with details that mattered?

I wonder now if I gave him white hair because of

the monster I did fear back then. The monster's name was Betaal, the ghost, and he showed up every Sunday afternoon on my parents' TV. He had thick white hair down to his shoulders, a red mouth, and an alabaster face. Directed toward young audiences, the show *Vikram Aur Betaal* (*Vikram and the Ghost*) was based on a two-thousand-year-old Sanskrit book, where Betaal was the spooky antagonist to Vikram, the righteous and handsome king.

As per the original story, Vikram's task is to retrieve Betaal from the cremation ground and bring him to the tantric or the sorcerer to fulfill a vow made earlier. But wily Betaal doesn't want to go. So, like Scheherazade from *One Thousand and One Nights*, he offers to tell stories to Vikram. However, there is a catch. The end of each story contains a riddle that Vikram must answer. If he doesn't know the right answer, Betaal will go with him quietly to the sorcerer. If he does know the answer but chooses to remain quiet, Betaal will come to know immediately, and he will kill Vikram. But if Vikram answers correctly, Betaal will return to his perch, and Vikram will have to try to nab him all over again. Needless to say, Vikram is able to answer all but the very last riddle.

Which is why each episode of the show began with Vikram, resplendent in orange silk and bejeweled necklaces, walking through the cremation ground in search of Betaal. Littered with skulls and bones, the only vegetation were dead trees from whose branches hung thick black snakes, watchful and dangerous. Fog and mist would roll in unexpectedly, and Betaal would loom into view, hanging upside down from the highest branch. Vikram would climb the tree, wrestle and finally overpower Betaal so he could carry him on his back. More than his hideously painted face, it was his wails and cackles that I feared the most.

And yet, I watched *Vikram and Betaal* regularly. It helped that Betaal disappeared after twenty-five minutes of airtime, leaving me, the satisfied viewer, with a new meaty story to mull over. To this day, I can recall his features clearly. If I stumble, there is Google to help and several old episodes uploaded on YouTube to refresh my memory.

But the man in the toy store cannot be found on the Internet. He has no name, no distinguishing features, nor a voice I can match to an identify-this-sound software. I cannot say for sure whether he had white hair. Perhaps it is immaterial. It is the one definite physical detail I have stamped on him, and it is what he will have forever—he, the monster I have to live with, the monster who will never disappear.

In the Land of Water: An Essay in Three Parts

Part 1: Touching Down
August 1, 2008

From the skies, Bangladesh looks like a wound. The patches of paddy fields and forests resemble soft welts submerged in grey bathwater. But when you lose some of the elevation, the same landscape reveals its one-of-a-kind loveliness and gives a sense of why so much of this country's poetry and music have paid tribute to its water-soaked beauty. With the plane's gradual descent, the bathwater transforms into a famished sea, its waves ravenous for the emerald-green land that looks frail and vulnerable. Strapped in an air-conditioned seat, I am still hundreds of feet away, but my eyes are trained on the window. I am a child of the tropics. I know the air down there must feel close and sticky, like swatches of glue pasted all over one's body, and for the skin to breathe, it has to work its way through several coats of sweat before it can reach the oxygen. I close my eyes and imagine what Bangladesh will smell like. Will it be warm and salty like seawater or old like nonstop rain? Or will it reek of decay and of moisture staining every seam?

I was born in Calcutta but raised in New Delhi, and I have imagined this journey every time my parents insisted that New Delhi was only a temporary arrangement and that we would eventually return to Calcutta, their hometown. That statement used to make me furious. I would argue that they could hold on to any illusion they wanted, but for my brother and I, home was and would always be New Delhi. I imagined this journey in my early twenties when I lived and worked in Chandigarh, the city at the foot of the Himalayas, where I tired of the same question again and again, "Where is your family from originally? You can't be from New Delhi. Bengalis are from Calcutta." I have imagined this journey a lot more in the last two years that I have spent in America, where I have had to rethink my answers for: *Who am I? What does it mean to belong to a country? Can one have more than one home?*

But most often, I have imagined this journey since the summer I turned fifteen. It was toward the end of June, and I was at my paternal grandparents' home in Calcutta for a two-month vacation. On that particular day, it had been raining since morning. Nothing unusual. It was the monsoon season, after all. Although humid, the air had a lightness to it that felt good on my skin. My grandmother and I had finished lunch, but neither of us was willing to leave the dining table. She had once again donned the mantle of the storyteller and I, of the greedy listener. Our right hands were crusting over with the telltale remains of the curries we had just devoured.

Since my arrival, this post-lunch story session had become our own sacred ritual. I loved listening to her stories of growing up in Fatehabad, a small town in the Chittagong district of present-day Bangladesh. But as much as I loved listening to her, nothing could have prepared me for the question she put to me that rainy afternoon. Without any preamble, my grandmother asked, "Did I ever tell you that your father was an unwanted child?"

Even now, so many years later, I remember the quietness of the moment, how surreal it felt, and the way the words fell out of her, unrestrained. My first thought was that I must have misunderstood. My grandmother was only telling me a story about a distant relative or a long-ago friend from the village. This could not be about her.

Someone so much in love with music and art and poetry must have wanted her first child, her son, my father.

My disbelief must have shown on my face. And so she repeated her words, "Your father was an unwanted child." I felt I was really seeing her as an individual for the first time. Up to that moment, she had only been my grandmother, a repository of both affection and discipline, a source of shrimp curries and stories. But now, she had transformed into a stranger. Someone with secrets, with a past, with motives and reasons I would never truly understand. What added to the uncanniness of the moment was that she spoke to me in English, a language we never use in our family to communicate with each other. Why should we speak English when we have access to Bengali, our melodious mother tongue?

My grandmother didn't wait for my response or a prodding, follow-up question. She switched to Bengali, and the details poured out, as if she had to tell it all in one afternoon. And worse, I had to be the one to whom she finally told her story.

"I was at my father's home in Fatehabad. The house was filled to capacity with visitors, but I felt alone. Probably because your grandfather was still in Calcutta. Not that he would have been allowed inside the birth room. Childbirth was strictly a women's-only affair. It was unusually cold for mid-October. The midwife, a bony, middle-aged woman, kept wiping my damp forehead with a towel. She had delivered nearly every baby in Fatehabad. By the light of the kerosene lamp, she looked blurry. By the time the baby arrived, it was dawn."

"Why was Baba an unwanted child?" I interrupted. I needed an answer, but I was not sure I wanted to hear it.

"Your grandfather and I had no money, no proper home. India had just become independent and partitioned into two: Hindu land and Muslim land. No matter where you went, there was always the threat of yet another riot. Our families were still angry with us for marrying against their wishes. Do you know my mother-in-law was so upset that her son had married *me*, this girl who did not belong to their caste, that the first time I walked into their home as a new bride, she greeted me not with the traditional ululation but with the wails of a mother who has just lost a child?"

I don't remember how long we lingered at the dining table that day. I know I didn't say much, nor did I ask her any more questions. I helped her clear the table, fold away the dining mats, and feed the fish bones to a motley of neighborhood cats who arrived at the same time every afternoon as if they had made a note of it in their planners. After she stashed the leftovers in the fridge, we went off to our respective bedrooms to nap and to read.

Later in the evening, as I stood on the balcony of my grandparents' home and watched the last rays of the sun bronze the eucalyptus trees in the distance, I kept hearing my grandmother's words. I felt betrayed by her confession. It was as if in one stroke, she'd orphaned my brother and me, destroyed my parents' existence, and reduced us all from a family to nothing.

I thought of the Bengali colloquialism my mother often quotes. *Blessed is the daughter who resembles her father.* Publicly, I had always denounced it as silly. Secretly, though, I loved it. I thought of the numerous times friends and family members had remarked on the similarities I share with my father—the same brown eyes, broad nose, wavy hair, dimples, some of our mannerisms, such as being short-tempered, able to live exclusively on a diet of meat, and sharing the same disdain for organized religion and religious fundamentalists. I thought of the few times I had been approached in a city of New Delhi's size and population by absolute strangers, curious to know if I was related to him. One of the inquirers had been his former colleague, the other an ex-classmate. In both cases, they had lost touch with my father over the years but were keen to reestablish it.

I thought of the cardboard village my father made for one of my school projects when I was in the third grade. It came with four huts, each with adjoining plots of paddy rimmed with coconut trees. In the center of the village square, there was a stepped well with a draw bucket fashioned out of the red cap of a toothpaste tube. I thought of my favorite game with him as a kid. We called it "Countries' Names," and it not only taught me the names of countries and their capitals but made me insatiably curious about the world. I couldn't even count the number of times he had taken me book shopping. I remembered the stories he had told me of his childhood, of how his curiosity in all things electrical made him take apart gadgets only to see how they worked, and how he built his first radio and started his stamp collection.

In my head, I screamed at the woman who had just taken it all away: *How dare you! How could you?* My mind took me to that house in Fatehabad in those twilight years of the 1940s. I imagined its people-filled rooms where discussions over the increasingly chaotic conditions of their newly-independent country must have churned the air like smoke. I sensed their ever-present fear of riots and saw the cold room in which a sweaty young woman gave birth by the shaky light of a lantern. I heard the midwife whisper words of encouragement and wipe her brow.

৩

And so here I am, at the age of twenty-eight, en route to Chittagong, Bangladesh's second largest city and biggest port. From the window seat of the tiny, 30-seater plane that I have boarded from Calcutta, my first impressions of Bangladesh can be summed up in a solitary word: *water*. I now have firsthand reason to understand why even a casual mention of Bangladesh, to a Western audience in particular, conjures up visions of typhoons, floods, and famines.

As I look at the deceptively gentle and placid landscape, I am reminded that Bangladesh is the largest delta on the planet. Because it has been blessed with the most intricate and generous network of rivers and tributaries—all of them originating in the Himalayas—Bangladesh also has one of the highest density of rivers in the world. But this claim to fame comes at a price and one that Bangladesh pays every year when river and ocean erosions wash away nearly twenty thousand acres of land, displacing about one million people. Like many other developing nations, Bangladesh contributes little to global warming but will suffer the most consequences. At present, between eighteen to twenty percent of the country's land lies within a meter of sea level, which places Bangladesh among the most vulnerable countries in the world, along with Tuvalu, Kiribati, Fiji, and the Maldives. In purely environmental terms, the vanishing of Bangladesh would mean the complete disappearance of the Sunderbans, which is the world's largest mangrove forest; the annihilation of the magnificent Bengal tiger; and the possible extinction of a few hundred bird, animal, and plant species. In terms of human loss, approximately thirty million people would be displaced, either directly because of the increase in water level or due to the loss of significant rice-producing areas.

But Bangladeshis are hardy, although it may be more on account of their circumstances than by choice. Years of being sandwiched between corrupt governments and natural disasters has made them capable of confronting everything with mind-numbing clarity and resilience. It is either because of this inbuilt mechanism or because Bangladesh isn't terribly advertisement-worthy that such apocalyptic projections aren't frequently discussed except among environmentalists.

But who am I to accuse anyone? I myself would not have confronted this dire truth had I not been flying over Bangladesh's aquatic skyline and grasped the unnerving reality of a country that is less land and more water.

The plane's wing dips sharply, and my stomach turns with the loss of altitude. I am reminded of the other threats facing this excruciatingly beautiful land—terrorism and religious fundamentalism. Which is especially unfortunate given the country's secular constitution, its tradition of a syncretic and tolerant Islam, and its citizens' deep regard for free speech and intellectualism. But Bangladesh is also one of the poorest countries of the world, and although this poverty does not breed terrorism on its own, it provides ripe conditions for wealthy foreign sponsors to set up shop and fund extremism.

Experts have noted that since its formal birth in 1971, Bangladesh has confronted one political crisis directly leading to another. Given the enormous density of its population, Bangladesh has also emerged as a perfect sanctuary for those needing to lay low or simply disappear. In the recent past, India has claimed there are terrorist camps here that not only spawn anti-India sentiments but also provide active military and economic support to guerrilla organizations operating in various parts of India, particularly its northeast, which shares porous borders with Bangladesh. This enables easy passage of men, money, arms, and ammunition.

There was a series of bomb blasts in India recently, which explains why the Calcutta airport was on high alert this morning and boarding the flight to Bangladesh became its own mini quest. It felt so forbidding in its fortified and militarized avatar that it reminded me of most large airports in America, where I have sometimes encountered ground staff suspicious of anyone with brown skin and a South Asian passport.

But my trip to Bangladesh is neither to investigate any terrorist organization nor to develop groundbreaking theories about global warming. My interest is purely selfish because Bangladesh is where I would have been born, this is where I would have been brought up, and its people are the people I would have lived with had it not been for the events of 1947, when both my paternal and maternal grandparents were forced to escape from this country and become refugees in the country next door, India. There, over a length of time, they peeled off one layer after another that identified them as immigrants, straightened the mismatched threads of their lives again, built new homes, and had their children and grandchildren, including me. In the process, they lost a language or two, some family, and several friends. But they also acquired, in their distinct ways, a somewhat constant need for permanence.

In my teens, I was impatient and restless. Fueled by romantic notions of travels and nomadism, I did not see the appeal of being rooted in one landscape. Yet I always felt a need for Bangladesh, the country my family had left behind. Even now, my gut instinct tells me that here I will instinctively feel at home because I will know all the flavors and spices of the local food, because I will be able to read the monolingual street signs, because of my familiarity with the sounds and syllables of the language, and because here no one will ask me, "So where are you from? Originally?" Who knows, perhaps here I will find the reason and motivation to dig permanent roots.

I tell myself to calm down. The story is in the details, and I have not been impressed by the few details I have seen of Bangladesh thus far. For example, the adventure at the Bangladesh High Commission last week when I went to get my visa. I had reached the offices very early, and yet, the lines outside the relevant counters were already sweaty, serpentine, and off-putting. Given the accents around me, it was clear most people were trying to pass themselves off as Indians. I wasn't buying it. "Illegal immigrants," I had muttered to myself, and not only had I cursed them for lengthening my wait time, but as the heat had progressed, dribbling down my forehead and dampening my shirt, I had begun to curse them for inundating India. Inquisitive eyes, that would not have considered themselves inquisitive, had decided to relieve their boredom by paying attention to me instead. They had peered over my shoulders, stared over my head, and gazed in rapt attention as I had struggled to steady the pen and paper and write my name, my address, checking off the appropriate boxes for gender, marital status, etc. When I had glared back, hoping that the gazers would be embarrassed enough to look away, their eyes had settled into mine with an expression conveying both politeness and puzzlement. Their stance was clear. They were saying to me, "And?"

Is the need for answers an essential characteristic of the subcontinental psyche? I am reminded of several conversations I have had in the recent past with my grandparents. Even though it is their hometown I want to visit, they have interrogated me and questioned my reasons. We have meticulously gone over maps and details, while I have tried to justify the fact that I need their story, because without its firm foundation, my own story cannot stand. In turn, I have acknowledged that I know I am appropriating their voices and their words, and I have wanted the reassurance that they are agreeable to that.

My grandparents are both in their eighties but extremely alert and active for their age. In addition to their real-world obligations, they have both been writers, so they recognize my need for this story. Yet, understandably enough, they are nervous that I am about to visit the country from which they were uprooted, where in the months immediately before and after August 1947, human rage assumed incomprehensible forms. It pulverized libraries and volumes of sacred literature into worthless powdery ash. It littered the streets in the name of religion with hacked bodies and limbs.

Since 1947, my grandparents have been to Bangladesh only once, and it's been twenty years since that visit. They are unsure of the Bangladesh of 2008, and the recent political crisis in the country has exaggerated their concerns. They have also told me that it might be unsafe for women to travel on their own, even in the streets of big cities, such as Dhaka and Chittagong, especially for those women who can be identified as unmarried or Hindu or Indian. I belong to all three categories, yet I feel brave, not because of any deep reservoirs of courage within myself, but because in Chittagong, I know that arrangements have already been made for me to live with some of our extended family members who did not migrate to India in 1947. They have been gracious enough to extend their home and hospitality to me while I conduct my research. I am intrigued by them and by the fact that in spite of sharing the same bloodlines, we need visas to share food around a common dining table or cook in each other's kitchen. Are they made of a tougher moral core that helped them decide to stay on and not give in to the pressure of migration when that's what most of their friends and family did in 1947 and for years thereafter? And why did they not migrate later when Bangladesh started showing the first signs of radicalization? Why did they not escape to the predominantly Hindu country that stood barely an hour's plane ride away? Was the lure of this land such that leaving it behind was never an option?

I turn away from the window to study the inside of this Bangladeshi plane. It looks like a more austere version of the kind of private planes in which Hollywood celebrities zip around to avoid paparazzi and attend secret weddings. At any moment, I half expect Victoria Beckham to pop out of the cockpit in a cloud of perfume, dangle a huge bag and a pair of oversized glasses, and let out a high-pitched "Surprise!"

In spite of the size of the plane, the lunch is fresh,

hot, and delicious. I devour the lamb biryani in minutes. The meat is browned just right, the rice has the perfect bite, and the accompanying spices have been measured out by an expert hand. The cucumber yogurt raita is ice-cold and lightly flavored with mint. It serves as a delicate partner to the robust biryani. I can't help but compare this feast to what's served on domestic flights in North America, where stewardesses offer juices and water with a kind of euphoria that is both uncomfortable and almost maniacal. In spite of being thousands of miles away from these flight attendants, my ears ring with their gushing-with-joy-high-pitched voices: "Would you like some cranberry juice or water?"

Last year, on a flight from Toronto, my fellow passengers and I were asked if we wanted to buy five-dollar lunch packages. We had had a choice between chicken sandwiches and a cheese and crackers platter. By the time they had reached my aisle, expectedly enough, the sandwiches were gone. Having been forced to buy the almost crusty and pallid cheese, I had spent the next hour trying to moisten its dryness.

This tiny aircraft has already taught me lesson number one—Bangladeshis have a definite idea about how to show they care. They feed.

৪০

I have landed. But I am neither breathing in salty seawater nor swabbing at a sweaty forehead. I do not feel instantly at home, although I *am* on Bangladeshi soil. Well, at least technically. I am still inside the airport—the Chittagong International Airport—and all around me is dry, air-conditioned perfection. Like its counterparts around the globe, this airport, too, is another conclave of luggage, lines, and bored airline staff. The cold steel structures are as aloof as the stairways and escalators, as business-like as the restaurants. I have been warned that because India is perceived as a land of plenty in Bangladesh, Indians are considered wealthy. Thus, by extension, a source of unlimited bribe. But in my case, the tag of "wealthy foreigner" is not only uncomfortable, it is a downright lie given my current status as an impoverished graduate student, who lives with a roommate, teaches a couple of classes, and works the maximum hours she can at her University's writing center to stay afloat.

On another level, it's confusing because ever since living in America, I have had encounters with people who have assumed suitably sympathetic expressions upon learning that I am from India. It's as if a part of their brain has beeped to them, in secret of course, "Remember not to ask about the poverty and the starving children. Instead, look happy, pious, and interested in her life. All at the same time."

The wall clock says it's 3:30 p.m., meaning 3 p.m. in India. I consider making a call to my grandparents to let them know that all is well here so far and that I have already been invited to dinner by two Bangladeshi families that were on the same flight with me from Calcutta. But I decide to hold off until my interview with the customs officer.

When it's my turn, he accepts my proffered passport and runs his fingers through his slight crop of oily, silver-grey hair. He has a small, almond-shaped head. As soon as he opens his mouth, I smell the tobacco and betel leaf. He doesn't have a full set of teeth, and the ones he has are stained a depressing shade of flax. But the smile does not leave his face, and he automatically becomes the first custom officer I have ever liked.

He starts with routine questions: "Is this your first time in Bangladesh?"

"Yes," I can't help but smile because this is the first time I am being interviewed in Bengali.

"And you are here for?"

I run the response in my head. Tourism is always the easiest and friendliest answer. "A holiday. I am here to meet family."

"Wonderful. Welcome to Bangladesh."

"Thank you."

"But otherwise you are from Calcutta?"

"I am coming from Calcutta, yes. But I am from New Delhi. My grandparents live in Calcutta."

"And what is this Idaho?"

"Yes, I live in Idaho."

"So you are not from New Delhi?"

I take a deep breath. "My grandparents live in Calcutta. My parents live in New Delhi, which is where I have lived most of my life. But since 2006, I have been living in the US, attending the University of Idaho. So right now you can say I have come from a combination of India and America."

"Very nice. Wonderful."

A mini crowd has gathered around my interviewer's chair. There are two janitors, a man and woman, and three male officers. They are in a circle, their elbows neatly balanced against the cubicle's top panel. Perhaps their break has coincided with my interview; perhaps they like to watch all interviews; perhaps they especially enjoy watching women's interviews. I am not sure.

My interviewer shoots another question, "And where in Chittagong are you going?"

"I will be in the city for a few days. And then I will head to Fatehabad. Do you know it? That's where my family is from."

"Of course I know it. Fatehabad is beautiful. But you have come at the wrong time of the year. It's the monsoons right now, the rivers are at their wildest."

"I am sure my family will know what to do."

He jots down some numbers, then reads something on a sheet. "Are you planning to purchase anything while you are here?"

"Maybe. I am not sure. Maybe some cotton saris for my mother and grandmother."

"Excellent idea. Wonderful, wonderful," he smiles affectionately, as if I am the daughter who has topped the annual exams yet again. I smile back but with caution. Why does he want to know what I might intend to purchase? Does he have a partnership with someone who owns and runs a store? Is he hoping to get a commission out of this whole deal?

But he forces me to set aside all my cynicism when he asks, "Do you have conveyance to go to your relative's house right now? Because if you don't, we can arrange your transport. You are from India, after all. You are our guest." The audience behind him, with their elbows placed next to each other and standing in compatible silence, nods and beams.

I am aware that airports are artificially constructed environments. They deal with a similar kind of paperwork, and for lack of a better term, humanwork, no matter their geographic location. There is perhaps nothing stunning or unique about their basic modus operandi, nothing that can distinguish one airport from the other aside from the amount of money they have at their disposal for security checks, machinery, and equipment. They are bound by a common need for discipline and punctuality, and for keeping tabs and accounting for numbers. Yet, nothing in this world gives a more accurate sense of a country and its people than an airport. And although kindness at airports is not rare, it's also not the most prevalent virtue—that would have to be the desire to keep things moving and fast.

But as I stare at my audience and at the customs officer in particular, I almost want to exchange phone numbers and friend him on Facebook. I hear myself say, "Thank you very much. Yes, my family will be here to pick me up. I am sure they are waiting outside. But just in case I cannot find them or I think I might get lost, I will get in touch with you for sure."

He smiles again, and as I walk away from his cubicle toward the exit, someone calls out, "Good luck in Fatehabad!" I turn back and wave. Then I push open the heavy glass doors and step out.

The visitors' area is packed, which makes sense given it's a Friday, and therefore the weekly holiday, the way it is in all Islamic countries. Several of the men are wearing the short rounded skullcaps, the kind favored by devout Muslims in many parts of the world. There are few women, and they are accompanied by male chaperones or cloaked in restrictive-looking black burqas, or both.

And here I am—standing by myself, without a veil and in high heels, dressed in a red that must be startling in its brightness and audacity. I am excited to hear the stories from this side of my family. I am eager to share

mine. I adjust the silk scarf around my shoulders and scan
the crowd for someone, anyone, who might call my name.

Part 2: Chittagong

Chittagong is the city of Chatgainya, the local dialect of the Bengali language, its words a mishmash of Sanskrit, Farsi, Arabic, and Portuguese. This melting pot is living proof of Chittagong's origins as a port town. In spite of a lifetime of speaking Bengali, Chatgainya comes to me only in bits and pieces. For the most part, it remains a mystery.

Chittagong is every shade of green. It's emerald so electric it hurts my eyes. It's jade, jungle, olive, lime, forest. It's mint, midnight, pigment, and pear. It's the smell of salt and shutki, the briny fish dried to sepia that every native eats as soon as she is old enough to cup a fistful of rice. It is the spicy snack of green gram, cilantro, and cardamom, best savored in the evenings with a cup of hot tea. It's the swirl of the bottle-green bushes outside the glass doors of the airport, the willowy trees with fragile, featherlike leaves that edge the coastline, and the coconut palms that defiantly shoot out of the city into its modest skyline.

It's the grass that carpets the land by the sea and the moss in the corners of dilapidated buildings. It's the green in the paddy fields, where farmers bent at the waist, plant one sapling at a time, and the fields of teenage boys engrossed in soccer, their wiry bodies taut with energy.

It's the sprawl of the Chittagong University campus. It is the roof of buildings, trims, and lattices, and that soft gleam of the city from its highest observation tower. It is the road signs and billboards, the egg-shaped, bristly jackfruits, and the pools of water that collect after every downpour. It is the cloth that covers the machines at every gas station, the painted body of auto rickshaws, the color of uniforms of police officers, the vinyl seat covers of bicycles, and the cotton fruits as plump as Indian gooseberries, their fatness an invitation to squish them, one satisfactory plop at a time.

It's the color of Islam that brings the country to rest on Fridays. It's the pillars of the grand mosque, the background of the national flag, and the graffiti that shouts all slogans—*Best Wishes this Festive Season, Stop Animal Brutality, May God's Grace Bless Us All.*

It's the border of my Bangladeshi aunt's cotton sari, and the gloss of the long-stemmed chili pepper she tucks next to the rice and fish on my lunch plate every afternoon. It's a simple gesture, instinctive and natural, and she does it without thinking, just like my mother and grandmother across the border in India.

৪০

The uncle who has invited me to stay with his family while I'm in Bangladesh is my father's first cousin. He is the eldest son of the family that continued to live in the ancestral home and didn't cross borders in 1947 to relocate to India. He thus belongs to the generation that has grown up exclusively in Bangladesh, unburdened by the baggage of straddling more than one culture. I am eager to hear his impressions of his country, of my country, and whether he feels any resentment toward his parents for their refusal to migrate. Is he content with where he is or does he, too, have the kind of nostalgia for India that I have for Bangladesh?

My uncle and his family moved to Chittagong city several years ago. They prefer the ease and convenience of an urban apartment with its access to all amenities of modern life. The ancestral home in Fatehabad is, for the most part, still intact. Portions of it have been rented out. A caretaker oversees the property, and my uncle pays supervisory visits every now and then.

It's my uncle and his son, my cousin, who pick me up from the Chittagong airport. The city rushes past us as we make small talk about my flight, travel plans, etc. Chittagong is a blur of traffic, Bengali billboards, and more men on the streets than women.

Partha, my cousin, is a handsome man, younger than me by a few years. He smiles easily, but in his dark eyes I sense a flurry of questions, "What are you here for exactly? Why have you come all this way from America to understand us? What do you need to understand? Why?" He watches me pull out my camera from the backpack and aim it at the city. "A picture of the dead and dying for your friends back in America, is it?"

I am stung by the question. But I catch Partha smiling. I can't be sure if he is teasing me or joking. I shake my head vehemently. "Of course not. I am only taking pictures of the city."

When I reach their apartment, my aunt ushers me inside with a hug. She is dressed in a kaftan-like outfit with a dupatta draped over her shoulders. She eagerly shows off her home and starts telling me about herself. I am already grateful for her hospitality. All I knew about her prior to this meeting was that she was a gifted singer and ran her own music school.

The drawing room provides the first glimpses into my family's history. Hanging from one of the walls is an enlarged photograph of Rajani Kanta Paul, my grandmother's grandfather, the patriarch of one of the wealthiest landowning families of Fatehabad. I have heard many stories about him from my grandmother. My favorite story is the time he received an invitation to attend Delhi Durbar, the celebration held in Delhi in 1911, to honor King George V and Queen Mary as the Emperor and Empress of India. King George was the sovereign ruler of Britain from 1910 to 1936, and therefore by extension, of almost half the world. Although in his personal life, the king was far more interested in collecting stamps than being in charge of administration, his coterie, headed by his jewelry-obsessed wife Mary, decided that his coronation had to be celebrated and his power demonstrated to as many luminaries as they could from all over India, the proudest possession of the British Empire.

I can only imagine the impact of the invitation when it reached tiny Fatehabad. After all, Rajani Kanta was going to meet, not an officer of the British Indian Army, not a local maharaja, not even the viceroy of India, but the King! The King of the World!

News like this was bound to spread and swell like a tidal wave, submerging everything else. Perhaps every morning when he stepped out to go to work, Rajani Kanta began to be followed by a mob of excited little children. Perhaps every afternoon as he sat down to eat his favorite dried shrimp curry with steamed rice, neighbors poured in, armed with sweets, gifts, and all kinds of requests. *Could we please see the invitation? May we touch it? Hold it?* Maybe, over innumerable cups of tea, they began seeking his opinion on matters as diverse as widow remarriage, ban on cow slaughter, and Hindu-Muslim unity. Overnight, Rajani Kanta may have become an expert on everything.

I know Rajani Kanta had a special garment stitched for the Delhi Durbar. It was an achkan, a long-sleeved, coat-like attire, traditionally favored by Muslim aristocrats of India. His achkan was apparently embellished with delicate gold threads and matching beads and sequins to make it truly worthy of the occasion. But he fell ill a few days before boarding the train that would have transported him from Calcutta, the nearest big city, to Delhi, the venue, and so his desire to meet the King remained unfulfilled.

I do not suppose King George V lost any sleep over Rajani Kanta's absence. Contemporary sources reveal that the crown he wore for the occasion contained over six thousand diamonds. The Queen wasn't far behind. She wore an emerald tiara and other matching jewelry. But the disappointment hit Rajani Kanta hard. For the longest time, he hung his beautiful unworn achkan inside his wardrobe, taking it out every now and then to run a light finger over the detailed embroidery. I assume he never stopped thinking about how it would have affected him, his family, and their standing in society had he indeed made it to the Durbar and been invited to a personal audience with the King. Maybe a photograph for the history books, or a personalized letter, or even a farman granting extra land rights or tax privileges.

But in spite of not making it to Delhi Durbar, Rajani Kanta did impact history. His most enduring legacy was his role as an educator and social reformer, particularly exemplified through his founding of the Fatehabad High School in 1894. This gesture, made to ensure that education could be available to everyone in Fatehabad irrespective of their socio-religious background, was not lost in the discrimination-seeped India of the 19th century, where education was restricted to a chosen few, usually the sons of aristocratic, high-caste families. Aware that for any change to be successful the initiative must come from within, Rajani Kanta enrolled his granddaughter, my grandmother, in the same school. And that is where she met my grandfather, and where in a sense, my story begins.

In his black and white photograph, Rajani Kanta is seated on a straight-backed chair. He is a slender man dressed in a white kurta, a matching well-pleated dhoti, and a white scarf whose two ends have come down from around his neck to fall on his chest. His shoulders are relaxed, his hands resting in his lap. His smiling eyes are focused somewhere above the photographer's head. Rajani Kanta has a full head of hair, a thick mustache, and a shy smile. His feet are ensconced in velvet slip-on shoes, and following the fashion of the times, worn without socks. A flower vase rests on the table next to him, and an uncurtained window imparts the photo with light. I can see the faint silhouette of a shadow through the window, but I can't tell what it is. Overall, the photo looks artificially enhanced, but still, I am grateful for it.

Diagonally across from this wall, sits Rajani Kanta's favorite chair. In Bengali, the word for it is *aaraam kedara*; literal translation, *the comfort provider*. And what a provider it is. The frame of the enormous lounge chair is carved out of teak, the seat is hammock-like but with the stability of a bed. It's a tried and tested, over-a-century-old La-Z-Boy. I imagine Rajani Kanta lying in it with his eyes closed, his fingers joined at the tips and held under his thin chin, making mental inventories of goods to be bought, land deeds to be secured, and taxes yet to be collected.

There are other smaller vestiges of that bygone era, emptied out of old decaying rooms and given a fresh burst of life and care. I see magnificent silver floor lamps with glass shades, the metal so pure and heavy that it's nearly impossible to lift them. Yet, in my mind, these lamps conjure up vivid images of a house being lit painstakingly, one wick at a time, the glow from a thousand candles brighter by that much because of reflections cast on silver.

These historical artifacts stand out in sharp contrast to the newer pieces of furniture—the fat sofas with red velvet upholstery, the crimson flowers in foot-long vases. In one corner stands an aquarium that may have once stocked fish, but now stores shells, both real and fake. There is a huge framed painting of Lokenath Brahmachari, the 18th century Bengali philosopher, and he is flanked by the Hindu god Shiva and his consort Kali, thus implying that Lokenath Baba (as he is known among his devotees) is the child of this divine union. On another wall, there is a battery-operated portrait of a Niagara-esque falls that glows and dims every alternate second.

There is also an enlarged photograph of Partha, my cousin. It's placed next to Rajani Kanta's. Dressed in opulent traditional clothes, the pleats of the dhoti just right, the kurta ironed to crisp perfection, his stance is unmistakably that of the feudal lord he would have been, were it not for independence and the dissolution of all forms of feudalism decades before his birth. I am tempted to ask Partha if he feels cheated, if he feels he will never get his due given the loss he has already incurred. His answer might surprise me. Maybe he will say that it does not matter to him at all and that he is truly a modern man, far removed from prejudices that create and impose discriminations. Maybe he will say he posed in that attire to make his mother happy or simply to have fun.

The dining room has the same profusion of large pieces of furniture. There is a six-seater dining table, though due to space constraints, only three spots get used at any point of time. The remaining chairs patiently wait their turn against a white wall.

When my grandparents fled, they had to accept the inevitability of their refugee status. They were rendered homeless and denied the secure lives they were once used to. But in the case of this branch of the family, their decision not to flee led them to the ignominy of living in a world that had once been built and perfected by their ancestors. All they could do was watch as it crumbled one piece at a time, one day after another.

ॐ

Although innumerable works of literature, art, cinema and scholarship have been devoted to examining the 1947 Partition of India, I want to utilize my time in Bangladesh to understand it from the point of view of scholars in Chittagong. How could an administrative plan conceived to grant political and religious freedom end up as one of the bloodiest and most significant events of the 20th century?

My first appointment is with Dr. Mishra, a well-known historian. I am traveling to his home with Sumesh, a part-time journalist and recent graduate of Chittagong University. Although he is friendly and unassuming, I don't want a chaperone, especially a man my age. But my aunt and uncle are convinced that Sumesh has an edge over me because he knows Chittagong thoroughly.

Last night when I had raised the subject of wanting to travel by myself, my aunt had said in protest,

"You look like a foreigner. You will be a target the moment you step out."

"How can I be a foreigner when I look exactly like everyone else?"

"Because your walk is different from that of the women here. It's urban. Aggressive."

"What if I carry only a little money? That way I won't care if I get robbed."

"It's not a question of money. You could be the target of something worse."

Which is why Sumesh is both my chaperone and bodyguard. He will not only escort me to Dr. Mishra's, he will safely bring me back as well. He has listened to my aunt's long list of dos and don'ts so cheerfully, I am positive that I am not his first charge.

Our mode of transport is one of those hundreds of auto rickshaws that skitter all over Chittagong. Our driver is guided by greater urgency than Alexander was to conquer the world. So we hold on to the sidebars as he barely avoids running over pedestrians and squashing stray dogs under his tires.

Chittagong is a city of slender people, their sizes that much more noticeable to me given my current residence in America, where I am learning to negotiate my way through humongous restaurant portions, sinful refills, and fast-food restaurants. I am also struck by how few women are out on the roads on their own. I can tell from the uniforms, a vast number of them are students en route to their schools and colleges. Others, dressed in saris or salwar kameezes, have covered their heads. A few have veiled their faces.

As we continue to drive, I think about how lucky I am that Dr. Mishra has agreed to see me on such a short notice. He has several books to his credit and rumor has it that since his retirement, he has begun working on another. I imagine he looks every inch the professor— silver-haired with a matching distinguished beard. He wears cottons that are either grey, blue, or white, and he ushers visitors into his study, where he sits on the same well-worn chair he has had for decades. The walls of his home must be lined with books of varying lengths and languages, their peeling spines the only indication of how long he has had them. His desk must be stacked with paper, from chapter drafts to photocopied articles to journals with colorful placeholders sticking out like feathers. His study must smell of ink, too much tea, coffee, or cigarettes, or all three of them, and the musty odor of books. I am comforted by the image of the cozy eccentric academic I have conjured up. I cross my fingers and hope Sumesh lets me do most of the talking.

When I ring the bell and Dr. Mishra opens the door, the only thing I have guessed correctly is the color of his hair. He is dressed in a faded blue lungi and a grey shirt, frayed at the shoulders. The inside of the apartment is balmy and smells of eggs, medicines, and windows that haven't been opened in months. Dr. Mishra seats us in his living room. It has an old couch, three aluminum chairs, and a divan with pillows untidily scattered about. Only one of the four walls is adorned with a picture—that of a spectacled young man—and the other three are bare. The floor hasn't been swept in days. There is an overall sense of melancholy, as if the room has accepted its deterioration. It knows it's pointless to fight against decay and that it's easier to live with the knowledge that furniture will disintegrate with time, floors will become grimy, walls will peel, and their colors fade.

Dr. Mishra tells us to make ourselves comfortable as he goes inside to get his reading glasses. Sumesh raises his eyebrows at me, then pulls out a large handkerchief from his pocket, dusts one end of the sofa, and sits down gingerly. Clearly I am not the only one with foolish ideas about how professors and their homes should look.

Dr. Mishra returns with his glasses but forgets to turn on the ceiling fan. Soon, what starts off as a discussion transforms into a teacher-student situation as Dr. Mishra slips into lecture mode. The Chittagong humidity is relentless and covers the three of us in sweat. Sumesh coughs and pointedly looks up at the fan. I discretely use my dupatta to blow some air in my direction. Neither of us wants to interrupt Dr. Mishra or offend him as he lectures on. He is so deeply involved with talking about June 3, 1947, when the plan to partition the subcontinent was agreed upon and made public, that he does not notice our discomfort. Ten minutes later, when it becomes apparent to me that a puddle of sweat will gather right between my sandals, I seek Dr. Mishra's permission and switch on the fan myself.

When I finally get a chance to explain to Dr. Mishra that I am a writer, not a historian, he shakes his head mournfully. "My dear, you cannot teach someone to write. Tell me, did Shakespeare ever go to a writing school? Can you become a historian? Yes, most certainly. Your personal story is not important. What did Partition do to this country? To all its people? That's the most important question. And as far as creative writing is concerned, I can assure you that this is just a way for your American university to make money at your expense."

I am reminded of all those voices of disbelief and

sarcasm back in India when I first announced my decision to study creative writing. In deference to Dr. Mishra's age and scholarship, I eat my words and bite my tongue.

In our hour-long meeting, Dr. Mishra is relentless in his attempts to steer the conversation more toward what he feels my research ought to be than what I want it to be. He recommends books that have been written on the Partition and criticizes newer works which lack, according to him, "authoritative scholarship." He is unimpressed by most modern historians, whether Indian, Bangladeshi or Pakistani. He tells me about the scholarly papers he has authored, the number of successful theses he has guided, and all those former students who stay in touch with him because their quest for higher learning is endless.

I sense how each of his comments is burdened by desperation, the kind I imagine every retired academic must feel—the fear of becoming obsolete and forgotten. Every time I politely remind him that I am in Chittagong to understand my family's and my own narrative, he waves a dismissive hand, saying good writers are intuitive creatures whereas good historians can be trained to excel.

Yet the Chittagong hospitality is still intact, as is the urge to feed. Within that one hour, Dr. Mishra gets up and goes to the kitchen twice and brings back large white bowls spilling with egg noodles and steel plates stacked with sweets, both of which have been prepared by his wife for us before she left for work that morning.

After we are done eating, Sumesh excuses himself to go to the bathroom. The moment he is out of sight, Dr. Mishra changes subjects. He asks me, "How old are you?"

I am taken aback by the question, but I answer, "Twenty-eight."

Dr. Mishra tilts his head toward the wall with the photograph. "That's my son. He would have been twenty-nine this year."

"What happened to him?"

"He died in a car crash six years ago. He was a student. In America."

The melancholy in this house finally makes sense. I understand its lethargy, its quiet acceptance of fate and decay. I tell Dr. Mishra, "I am sorry for your loss, Sir. What was he studying?"

Dr. Mishra smiles. "Not history, I can tell you. He had no patience for it. He was going to be an engineer. We knew he would be a good one. But then that accident... He used to say, 'Historians are stuck in a time warp. The future of the world lies in marching ahead, not looking back.'"

I smile, too.

Dr. Mishra continues, "Earlier when I was at the University, the days just zipped by. Students, seminars, faculty meetings, book discussions, PhD theses, protest marches. There was no time to miss anyone. Not that I am not busy anymore. I am. Ever since my retirement, I have been working on a new book on the history of contemporary Bangladesh. Nothing too far back. One that I think my son would've enjoyed reading."

Sumesh comes back and Dr. Mishra switches topics again. It's time for us to leave, but Dr. Mishra invites me to come another day so I can meet his wife and tell her about my life in America. Although Sumesh is in the room with us, Dr. Mishra looks only at me. Clearly the invitation does not include chaperones.

We thank Dr. Mishra and take his leave. Compared to his living room, even the big-city, polluted air smells clean, and my salty skin feels refreshed. Inside the auto, Sumesh has to scream so I can hear him over the traffic. "Do you think you will see Dr. Mishra again?"

"I don't know. I have to think over it."

"If you want to see him again, you will have to come by yourself. He is not interested in me, the part-time journalist. You do realize Dr. Mishra is not interested in you for your sake? He is only trying to relive his career as a history professor."

I shrug. I am eager to return to my home here, my uncle's apartment. I have grown accustomed to its routines, to the sounds and flavors of my aunt's cooking, to Partha zipping in and out to attend classes, and to my uncle returning from his office at a set time every evening.

When we finally arrive, the apartment smells of fried fish and hot chilies sautéing in the frying pan. I can hear the basmati rice bubbling in the pressure cooker. Partha is out with friends. My aunt invites Sumesh to stay for lunch. Soon after we eat, the apartment will fill up with my aunt's music students. They will seat themselves on floor rugs and form a semi-circle around her. She will peel the cover off the harmonium and for the next hour or so, the walls will resonate with rich clear notes of traditional Bengali songs, the ones my parents and grandparents love, the very same songs that I once disliked as a teenager but now listen to in America.

Sumesh doesn't stay for lunch. He has other business to tend to. I thank him profusely, but we don't bring up the topic of Dr. Mishra again.

৪০

"Are you familiar with the story of Zamor, the

Bengali boy captured from Chittagong by slave traders and sold to the French, who eventually ended up in the household of Comtesse du Barry, the mistress of Louis XV?"

"Wait, Louis XV? THE Louis XV?" I can't hide my incredulity. I am in the living room of my uncle's apartment in conversation with one of Chittagong's senior journalists, Jamaluddin Chaudhury. A devout Muslim, Jamaluddin writes predominantly in Bengali, and his subjects encompass current affairs, religion, and social problems. Jamaluddin has a gentle, yet authoritative and measured way of speaking that convinces me he has a researcher's zeal for stories and a historian's compassion for all those stories forgotten or misunderstood.

"Yes, Zamor was eleven years old when he was kidnapped. He was trafficked from Chittagong to Madagascar. Once he reached France, he was christened Louis-Benoit. The Countess thought he was African, and she was so entertained by the fact that his language sounded nothing like French that she had him displayed as a curiosity. Nevertheless, she was affectionate toward him. Later in life, though, Zamor participated in the French Revolution and betrayed the Countess. At the trial, he cited Chittagong as his place of birth. The Countess died at the guillotine."

"What happened to Zamor?"

"He worked as a school teacher for a while. He died a poor man."

I show Jamaluddin the books I have thus far purchased in Chittagong. Most of them are on the modern history of Bangladesh. Jamaluddin discusses their recurring issues and raises an important point, "It's wrong for historians to blame the migration of Hindus out of East

Pakistan on Muslims alone. The real factor was the fear instilled by those Hindus who were outside and had endured riots, such as the Great Calcutta Killing of 1946. It was they who convinced their brethren here that East Pakistan was not safe for them."

I ponder over the veracity of Jamaluddin's claim. I have seen photographs of the Great Calcutta Killing—the dead and wounded sprawled amid rubble and waste, the faithful bent in prayer, an armed mob, children hiding behind livestock, military tanks rolling in formation, upturned rickshaws on the road with wheels like the eyes of a mythical monster, and streets that look as if they've just been washed in blood or water—it's impossible to know for sure in the black and white photographs. Aside from the fact that the rioters and their victims are dressed according to the sartorial dictates of the 1940s, the photos can belong to any decade and part of the country, be it Gujarat, Delhi, or Uttar Pradesh.

The Great Calcutta Killing occurred exactly a year before Independence. Over 4000 people died within a span of 72 hours, and nearly 100,000 were rendered homeless. More than any other event, it was this one in particular that set the wheels in motion for Partition. It pushed the demand for a Hindu-majority India and a Muslim-majority new state, Pakistan, both of which would come into existence after the British Government handed over the reigns of power.

My grandparents were students in Calcutta during the Great Calcutta Killing. They lived in hostels separated from each other by several miles. On that day, August 16, 1946, both of their hostels were attacked by angry violent mobs. Both of them were caught unawares. They fled with their friends. My grandfather had no money in his pocket.

The older brother of one of my grandmother's friends acted as the girls' chaperone. They didn't return to their hostels for the next few days. They stayed off the streets, hiding from mobs, switching from one safe house to another, and living on the hope that the other was safe.

Maybe it was the Great Calcutta Killing that more than anything else steeled their decision to leave Fatehabad forever. They didn't want to risk being the minority. They chose, instead, the relative comfort of trying to blend with the majority even if it came with the tag of *refugee*.

৪১

It's been seven days since I landed in Chittagong, and my cousin Partha and I have become friends. Gone is his wariness and suspicion. There is comfort and ease in our language, in the way he addresses me as "Didi," the Bengali for Big Sister, and in our acceptance of each other as siblings almost. We have lingered over shutki dinners and stayed up late to chat or watch Hindi films on TV. We have bonded over our love for food, our skepticism of religion, our criticism of our countries' politics, and our curiosity about the world. Partha has introduced me to his girlfriend and his favorite roadside snacks. He has accompanied me to the local museum, given me a tour of Chittagong University, and driven me to any number of bookstores. Together, we have spent some excellent afternoons teasing his mother for her fear of the ocean and all sea creatures, mythic or real.

Today, we are out on the beach. It's early evening and as we lower ourselves on the gigantic black rocks rimming the water, I can't tell which way is east or west.

The sky is uniformly cloudy and streaked with alternating shades of grey, steel, and silver.

Partha is telling me about the many varieties of chilies in Bangladesh, including a misleading white one. When it was first discovered, the locals were so taken in by its milky skin, they named it Sahib Marich or White Man's Pepper. In spite of its beguiling color, Partha assures me that one bite is enough to invoke the heat and fury of hell.

From where we have settled down on the rocks, our view of the Bay of Bengal is neither clear nor uninterrupted. Ships and trawlers, with names both local and foreign, have dropped their anchors. I don't mind. This scene is still very new to me. Partha hums a Hindi song, and I sense the growing heft in the air. It's the promise of yet another downpour. I think of my other home, the typical graduate student apartment I share with my roommate in Idaho. Our neighborhood has tall pine trees and tiny yards strewn with cones and acorns. They serve as constant physical reminders of how far away I live from the tropics. Just before a storm, the air there, too, smells dense and electric, and once the rain passes, it stays clean and fresh given its relative closeness to the mountains.

"Have you heard of mochabhati?" Partha asks.

I shake my head.

Partha begins his history lesson. "I am not sure how popular they are now, but long ago, say when our great grandparents were young, sailors and fishermen who set off from Chittagong relied on mochabhati. First you boiled the rice, then drained it, and while the rice was still hot, you molded it into a tight compact ball. You wrapped it in many, many overlapping layers of banana leaves so the rice stayed nice and fresh under this thick armor. Once at sea, fishermen could break a chunk off the rice, add it to a curry of their choice, and have a spicy satisfying meal in minutes."

One of the things I learned from my grandfather before landing in Chittagong was that sampans, the local, flat-bottomed wooden boats, are originally from China. A *sam pan* literally means *three planks* in Cantonese. But their easy design and simple construction made them so popular that they became native. I imagine the fishermen on one such sampan, exhausted from a whole day of netting, capturing and storing fish, settling down to a well-deserved meal against the setting sun. They light a few hookahs that envelop them in a smoky intoxicating haze. The "cook" takes out the shutki from inside a dry box. He washes the dried and cured fish several times to get rid of most of its salt. The youngest boy in the crew is assigned the task of slicing red onions, a stick of ginger, and a handful of green chilies. The cook fries the ingredients in a wok. When they start to brown, he adds a generous pinch of pepper and turmeric. No one has taught him the fussiness of measuring spoons. Someone remembers that he has a whole eggplant in his bag. He brings it out, and the unexpected treat is greeted with joy and added to the wok. The shutki goes in last, once the vegetable softens. Soon, greedy-hungry fingers dig into the ostrich egg-sized rice balls they have brought from home, and with the very first salty-fiery bite, the aches of their long hard day are lessened if not forgotten.

Partha and I are both quiet. He is probably lost in thoughts of his classes or his girlfriend or something innocuous, like what to watch on TV tonight. Any moment now, he will tell me it's time to go home. I am still thinking of sampans.

When I first arrived in Chittagong, our blood ties were all that connected Partha and I. But now there is more. The sense of our shared loss, our common country, and the divisive history our families must continue to bear.

"Come on, Didi," Partha says, scrambling to get a firm foothold on the slippery rocks. He offers me his hand. "Let's go before Ma calls the army, navy, and air force to report we have been kidnapped by the pirates of the Bay of Bengal."

Part 3: Fatehabad

It's a sunny Friday morning, the kind where you want to gather friends and go out to brunch, but Bangladesh is quiet and resting. Fridays are national holidays. They are what everyone looks forward to after the week's fatigue. Around noon, many will step out to answer the call for congregational prayer, the jum'ah, and the streets will explode with sound and color and the thrum of thousands united in prayer.

Right now, however, the streets are empty, and my uncle and I are taking advantage of this fact by speeding toward Fatehabad. Our auto rickshaw driver is also a Fatehabad native and known to my uncle's family for decades. Although the two men are not friends, there is an easy familiarity between them and in the way they exchange words and consult over the shortest route to take.

I adjust my dupatta as I settle into the auto. I am nervous for reasons I cannot explain well. I do not know what to expect in Fatehabad. What if Fatehabad leaves me disappointed? What if this encounter that I have imagined and re-imagined turns out to be the biggest let down of my life? What if this highly romanticized back-to-the-land movement only brings me the hostility of people who might question my very right to be here? So what if once upon a time my ancestors lived on this land. They were evicted more than sixty years ago. How can I possibly try to reclaim something that did not belong to even my own father?

But I know I am in good hands. My uncle knows everyone in Fatehabad. More importantly, everyone knows him. Despite the government's abolition of titular and hereditary institutions, his specialness remains unchanged though the obvious trappings of aristocracy have long ceased to exist. When the same logic is applied at the national level, it's easy to see why dynastic politics are so inbuilt in the South Asian psyche.

The auto rickshaw phut-phuts its way through roads flanked by coconut trees, puddles of murky monsoon water, tall grasses, stray dogs, and small stores that sell odds and ends but whose shutters are down today. It never ceases to amaze me how deliciously cool the Chittagong breeze feels on my skin. If only I could just bottle it and carry with me everywhere. If I could take the road signs, that would be even better. I know I will miss seeing the Bengali script once I am back in Idaho, where I will once again be surrounded by the monotonous singularity of English.

ॐ

Fateh means *victory* in Persian, however, Fatehabad, *the land of victory* was never the epicenter of battle. Then why the arrogance of this name? Because sometime in the 18th century, the industrious ruler of Bengal, Murshid Quli Khan, appointed a new local subedar. His name was Fateh Khan, and he took himself and his job seriously. To appease his ego, the locals renamed the village in his honor. And so, in spite of never having waged a war nor the bittersweet glory that comes with it, the villagers became the proud residents of *the land of victory*.

Like any good piece of land, Fatehabad, too, is layered with stories. They speak of its ability to provide, sustain, endure. Its rocks, trees, and rivers tell stories of those born and raised here. They inhaled its dust, rubbed it out of their eyes. They sat ankle-deep in its water, plucked its wildflowers, chased its fat earthworms. Other stories are owned by visitors, whether they lived here for a handful of days or were merely passing through, whether they were real or imaginary.

I have heard the story of the haunted pond countless times from my grandfather, a skeptic. Apparently, the pond is frequented by the ghost of a young wife who sits by the water every night and weeps into her cupped hands. For as long as she lived, she was tortured by her husband. He would tie her up, hurl food and stones at her, and give confusing directions for household chores. When she failed at them, he punished her severely. In the last rainy season of her life, she caught a fever. By then her husband had lost all interest in her and was keen to marry someone else. He hired a quack to poison her. After three days of unbearable pain, the wife died in her sleep, but incessant monsoon rains meant she couldn't be cremated immediately. The woods were wet. Her corpse, wrapped in red—she had died a wife, after all, the highest honor—lay unattended for three days. By the time her husband set her on fire, her body had decomposed horribly. Soon locals began to claim they had spotted her beside the pond she used to frequent. Some insisted she had folded her hands, asking for help. Three months later, on the eve of his second wedding, the husband suffered mysterious burns while lighting something as innocuous as his hookah. He died, begging for water.

ॐ

The auto rickshaw sputters to a stop outside my grandmother's childhood home—a two-story mansion the color of brewed tea and sepia. There are patches of overgrown grass and tall columns that haven't seen a fresh coat of paint in years. Some of the walls are stained black, as if a giant flailed about, slapping this brick and that with dirt-smeared hands. Where manicured bushes once encircled the house, now they are each their own jungles. Every exposed brick has layers of moss, as do the boundary walls, like patches of green carpets left to dry. On a far wall, a shirt hangs from a nail, its frayed sleeves awaiting the return of its owner.

The house has a temple on the grounds. Dedicated to the family gods, its four steep steps lead into an arched entrance. While the house does not show any visible sign of activity, two priests bustle about the temple supervising morning prayers to the clutch of devotees that have gathered. A cadence of Sanskrit mantras fills the air as one of the priests holds up an earthen lamp to the deity's face.

We are welcomed inside the silent mansion by the caretaker. A large bunch of keys jangles from his right hand. He looks to be in his forties, and from the way he and my uncle talk to each other, I can tell he has held this job for years. He is a small slender man dressed in a camel shirt and a brown-black checkered lungi. He has a full mustache and a pale shadow of a beard. With his keys and knowledge of this mysterious house, he reminds me of the archetypal mentor character in stories—Gandalf in *The Lord of the Rings* or the fairy godmother from *Cinderella*.

I follow them into the first room. It smells of moss, wool, and damp walls. The shuttered doors and windows, although still gorgeous in design and strong in construction, haven't allowed the sun inside for months. The ceilings are cavernous, the walls solid, and I can't help but smile imagining my grandmother weaving in and out of these rooms—as a little kid running with her sisters in their pursuit of fruits from the orchard; then as a young girl walking to school lost in thoughts of friends and classes; a few years later, departing for Calcutta for her bachelor's degree; then returning, as a wife and would-be mother, to the comfort of this familiar world to give birth to her son, my father.

I walk into other rooms, just as spacious and quiet, bereft now of both furniture and ornamentation. But once upon a time, these rooms buzzed with people. They entertained and celebrated, fought and quarreled, and embraced the daily business of life's sundry demands. The mood of the mansion is such that I am reminded of *The Hungry Stones*. Published in 1916, it is one of the most loved short stories written by the Bengali Nobel Laureate Rabindranath Tagore. The story's ominous-ambiguous quality is not dependent on whether one reads it in English or Bengali. Both are equally haunting.

The story begins with the narrator and his friend encountering a stranger, a renaissance man, who impresses them with his vast knowledge and expertise on numerous subjects. He tells them of the time he worked as a collector of cotton duties in Barich. His living "quarters" were a 250-year-old marble palace, now uninhabited, but once occupied by a king and his harem. Ignoring the warnings of an old clerk in his office, he settled into his new residence. The first few days passed without incident. One evening, however, as the collector sat admiring the sunset, he smelled fresh henna and rose ittar, the intoxicating smells one would expect to find in a medieval harem. Laughter rang in the air along with the tinkle of anklets and cheerful voices. He could not see anyone. But he felt them. The disembodied voices couldn't see him either, but they accepted him as part of their new reality.

With time, the collector grew obsessed with the palace and its invisible residents. So much so that he discarded his modern clothing in favor of traditional attire more becoming of feudal lords. He began staying up late to participate in the tableau of events that unfolded around him. He lost interest in his day job. He reached a point where he came to believe the stones of the marble palace were seeped with the memories of those who once lived within its walls. Those long-departed residents were still hungry for life and its sweet riches. By the end of the story, the reader is left to wonder if the collector himself is real or whether he, too, belongs to a forgotten turn of history.

ॐ

I follow my uncle into what used to be Rajani Kanta's office. I imagine my grandmother running in here to see him, her beloved grandfather. The room bears only one remnant of him. It is a metal cabinet, its skin a mosaic of green paint and rust, and its heavy lock, a protection from prying eyes and inquisitive hands. The rust makes the faint numbers on the lock impossible to read. An ornate brass plaque, the size of a cigar case, is embedded at the top right corner. Its three lines read:

Rajani Kanta
Fatehabad
Chittagong

Here in this room, he poured over ledgers, balanced books, and settled accounts. I have heard stories about the dubious nature of some of these transactions. Sometimes, his interest rates were too high and the terms inscrutable. Their purpose was to grab land, even if it rendered impoverished farmers homeless. But I have also heard stories of Rajani Kanta's generosity—that his wealth supported freedom fighters on the run and adopted families that lost loved ones to the national cause.

Instead of the reverence I expect to feel at that moment, I am overcome by rage. The indignity of displacement has never been more real. I am furious about the refugee tag that got tacked to my grandparents' identity. I cannot fathom the enormity of the decision they were forced to make—should they continue to risk living in Fatehabad or relocate to the new India and face an uncertain future there? I am angry that someone dressed in a uniform, a forced smile, and the inauthenticity inbred in most bureaucratic promises, showed up at the doorstep to inform them that the land, which had been theirs for five, seven, nine generations, was no longer theirs. I am numbed by the realization that such indignities are every day occurrences even now.

I ask my uncle, "Did you ever feel the urge to migrate to India?"

"No. But my parents did. And not just in 1947. We had to escape for a few months in 1971, during Bangladesh's freedom struggle. We lived with your grandparents. I was a ten-year-old obsessed with cricket. Your father was an engineering student. He lived away from home. I didn't see him very often."

As a country, Bangladesh is young, merely thirty-seven years old. After Partition, this former part of India came to be known as East Pakistan. While West Pakistan spoke Urdu, grew wheat, and had a more rugged topography, the East spoke Bengali, grew rice, and had a tropical climate. Still, it was assumed that the two parts would get along seamlessly because Islam, their common faith, would tie them together.

That did not happen. There were conflicts over unequal distribution of resources, sharing of political power, and the constant undermining of one language over the other. Bengali nationalism received support from India and after the fierce bloody revolution of 1971, East Pakistan separated itself from the West and rechristened itself Bangladesh, the Land of Bangla (Bengali), where the word represented the people as well as their language.

The caretaker leads us to the top floor. The narrow steep steps remind me of Mughal monuments that abound in Delhi and other parts of north India. Most of the space here is taken up by a terrace. There are only a handful of rooms. Irrespective of the direction I face, I see trees dressed in every shade of green arching for the blue of Fatehabad's sky.

The terrace floor is unlike any I have seen. It's undulating like waves. When I look at my uncle quizzically, he explains, "So that rainwater does not collect on the roof and seep down into the ceilings. See those matchbox-like holes along the terrace walls?" He points with his fingers. "They are separated from one another by roughly two feet, and they correspond with the points where the floor dips. This is how the drainage system works. Smart design, don't you think?"

I squat to photograph the rise and fall of the floor, the ornate railing, and the thick mesh of trees that protected the women of this house when they walked the terrace, away from the prying eyes of the world beyond.

Once we are downstairs again, my uncle leads me down a long, dimly-lit corridor until we reach a plain, non-descript room. Its bare walls have a green sheen. Unimpressive. Empty. It doesn't even contain a chair. Just as I am about to ask what's special about this room, my uncle says, "This is where your father was born."

My stomach clenches. I am fifteen again. I am sitting across from my grandmother at her dining table in Calcutta. The turmeric gravy has crusted on my hand, and I can hear the sentence that started it all and brought me here, "Your father was an unwanted child."

So this is where she lay on that unusually cold October night. And this is where mother and child remained for the next few days, while friends and family descended to see the newborn, argued over which of his parents he resembled. This is where my grandfather held his first-born and with not a coin to his name, blessed him with the gold medal he had just won at college.

My cell phone does not work here. I cannot call my father and tell him where I am. I make do by photographing every inch of this damp room. I stop when my uncle places his hand on my shoulder. "Enough," he says, "Let's visit your grandfather's home."

৪০

The monsoons have wrecked the streets that separate my grandfather's home from my grandmother's. We elect to walk. It's a short distance anyway. We pass a temple. On its stone steps sits a young priest on his haunches, polishing brass lamps that he probably uses for worship. His movements are brisk yet meticulous, the assured work of someone who knows what he's doing. His fingers are lined with rings, each studded with precious stones to appease gods and mollify planets so he can have a semblance of control over his life. He is clad in a customary white dhoti. His upper body is bare, except for the sacred white thread that bisects his torso. He looks up as we walk past. Since priesthood in Hinduism is a father to son prerogative that can be enjoyed only by Brahmins, I wonder if he is the descendant of one of the village elders my grandfather picked arguments with in his lifelong rejection of gods and faiths.

Unlike the lavish and sturdy mansion my grandmother called home, all physical remnants of my grandfather's modest home are gone. I am not standing on a clean floor that has been swept and tended to in anticipation of guests. My hold on this piece of wetland is precarious at best. One careless step, and I am done for. The mud settles in the seam of my clothes. It clumps to my sandals and weighs me down.

The grass is lime, gold, and green. Its blades shimmer like silk. A knot of banana trees stands in a circle, guarding the secrets of this site. Wind has bent their trunks until they have bowed in submission. Their branches are stretched like wings, and the long waxy leaves are folded in, making the trees appear shy and reserved.

There is no kitchen here anymore, no earthen jars of multicolored aromatic spices, no heaps of vegetables waiting to be cut and peeled, no stacks of just-caught fish, their eyes glassy in death. No clay oven burns in the corner, its flames reaching out from amidst carefully laid bricks, ready to cook another pot of rice. There is no grind of the mortar and pestle, nor is my great grandmother bent at the waist pounding whole spices, while intoning under her breath one of the thousands of shlokas that make up the *Ramayana*.

I don't see the baithak khana, the drawing room where my great-grandfather received visitors and held discussions on Keats and Byron. I imagine the rooms where guests lived for months, the lines of their lives blurring, intersecting, and smudging with those of their hosts. There are no traces of magnificent trees with gnarled trunks. I cannot reach out and pluck their fruits nor run my hands over blood-orange hibiscus in full bloom.

I don't see a puja room. No Brahmin priest has gathered here this morning, his hands neatly folded in front of him, to lead the Dasgupta family and their guests in prayer. I don't hear the clang of brass bells or the chanting of the sacred Sanskrit mantras. I can't smell the warm breath of incense as it fuses with the mild scent of the hibiscus or the clean bathed smell of the bodies standing next to each other in quiet devotion. I want to taste—but I can't—the sweet offerings of ripe litchis, papayas, and mangos made to the gods, and once sanctified by them, distributed among us, the mortals.

There is nothing in this banana grove to indicate a library stood here once, that it contained books written in three very different languages, and that rare books were added to it continuously. Very romantically, I wish for a leaf from an antique text to appear before me, its yellowed, dog-eared corners bearing a name I will recognize, a handwriting that will somehow preempt mine.

But I allow myself to see a boy. He is seven years

old. He loves books more than any games or pranks his friends can devise. He is stretched out on a bamboo mat on the floor of the library, one hand gripped around a book, the other cupping his chin. His white dhoti has an indigo stain or two—residues from his fountain pen and its leaking nib. His black hair is thick and wavy, and there is, as yet, no trace of the glasses he will start wearing soon. It's another humid afternoon in Fatehabad. But even as sweat gathers on his brow and neck, he turns his pages and reads on.

He cannot be distracted by the busyness of his home. All he cares about are these books his father has collected with care to improve upon the collection started by his father, a record keeper in the district magistrate's office, and his grandfather, a noted physician of Ayurveda.

I want to reach out to that boy and warn him that this library he loves so dearly will soon be gone. He will lose friends he values, and this land that he and his forefathers have been so deeply tied to for generations will be cleaved away.

"We should go now," my uncle says, pulling me out of my reverie. A significant part of my pilgrimage will end the moment I walk away from this piece of land, but I know we have one more place to visit. It will be my final stop. We board the auto rickshaw, and from its open windows, I watch the village shrink in size until it vanishes from my view.

ॐ

In the year 1894, the world saw the establishment of the International Olympic Committee, the enthronement of Russia's newest czar, Nicholas II, and the enforcement of the first minimum wage law in New

Zealand. In Fatehabad, Rajani Kanta laid the foundation of Fatehabad High School and enrolled his granddaughter, my grandmother. She was one of the school's nine female students. Although the remaining students were all boys, the very presence of these girls was a revolution by itself. The girls were under tremendous pressure. Not only did they have to uphold the fine progressive reputation of their own families, but they had to be models of discipline and good behavior so they could inspire other families. They knew that the slightest hint of slander would derail the impetus for female education and set it back by a decade or so.

The school, too, had to do its part. A strict set of rules was put in place to ensure the girls mingled only with each other and were safe from the gaze of their male classmates. After every class period, they were escorted by the teacher into the headmaster's office. In the security and sanctity of that august room, they waited until it was time for the next period, when the teacher in charge would come, collect them, and escort them back into the classroom.

శు

It's been sixty-eight years since my grandmother first walked through the gates of Fatehabad High School. Today I am at the very same spot with my uncle, also an alumnus of this institute. The motto inscribed in black against a pale cement background reads, *Spread the Light of Enlightenment*, in Bengali. The school insignia is equally apt—an open book with a glowing lamp reflecting its light on the pages.

The school is closed because it is a Friday. There are no students, staff, or faculty milling around. A solitary guard, with a thick beard and a white cotton cap, sits behind the gates reading a newspaper. He looks up, recognizes my uncle, and breaks into a smile. Wordlessly, he slides off his chair and unlocks the gates. He looks to be fifty-something but has a beard full of tight wiry curls. In the guard's salaam, it is once again evident that he does not see my uncle for who he is at present—a regular man with a regular desk job—but the great-grandson of Rajani Kanta, the founder of the school, the once feudal landlord of Fatehabad.

My uncle is a good-natured, gracious man. He has grown up knowing these privileges, but he does not treat them lightly. He acknowledges the guard's greeting then inquires about his family. He introduces me and explains the purpose of my visit.

The guard salaams me as well. "How do you like your village?" he asks.

The pride in his voice reminds me of a conversation I had with one of my American professors shortly before I left for Bangladesh. We were sitting in his office, looking at photographs of his recent trip to Tibet when he said, "It's hard to express the pride Tibetans feel about their homeland. I have never met another group of people so happy and thankful for where they live. The Tibetan shepherds and yak herdsmen endure such hard lives, especially in the winter, when there is not a spot of green on the Himalayas, and yet every time I ran into one of them and was asked where I was from, they were full of sympathy at learning that I was not from Tibet. They felt genuinely sorry that I wasn't from the 'most beautiful place on earth.'"

I return the guard's salaam. "It's so green. Everything is beautiful. I will need more than one trip to see everything."

"You must take your time, and you must see it all before you go back. Or maybe we can just keep you here forever." The guard waves his hand towards the school. "I cannot open any of the classrooms. I don't have those keys."

We assure him that's not a problem. At least I can walk through the school grounds, jot down notes, and take a few pictures. He returns to his perch, dives back into his newspaper. As I look around me at the one-story building where my grandparents were once students, at the long-pillared corridor where the classrooms are placed next to each other like an assembly line, and at the serene lake sunk right inside the school grounds—my family's story seems more real than ever. It's tangible. It has concrete beginnings and ends, an actual landscape, a context for each of the characters and their individuality.

The classroom windows are tightly shut, but I still try to peer inside. One day, in one such room, my sixteen-year-old grandfather had stumbled upon the words "I love Minati," chalked in bold letters across the blackboard. It was the handiwork of one of her many secret admirers. But such declarations of love were too forward. Impolite. They hurt the girl's reputation. My grandfather, enraged with the offender's audacity, had scrubbed the blackboard clean.

For reasons only known to him, he had kept the blackboard incident a secret for almost sixty years of their marriage. It stumbled out only recently during the handful of days when I was in Calcutta right before I left for Bangladesh. The night the secret revealed itself, we had finished dinner, but true to habit, were lingering over our empty plates. That's when my grandfather shared the story. I remember the matter-of-factness of his delivery, and yet his words embarrassed my grandmother. I could see the silent imploration in her eyes. "What are you doing? Must you tell such inappropriate stories to our granddaughter?"

The memory prods me to look for the headmaster's office, where female students were corralled to make them feel safe. But teenagers, irrespective of time, nationality, or religion, always find ways to defy rules, and I know my grandmother was no exception.

The headmaster's office had glass windows that overlooked the sports fields. Most mornings, the boys would be there playing football. For the girls, stepping out to watch the game was out of the question. So they devised a plan, aided by the fact that the headmaster himself taught a large number of classes and wasn't always available to keep an eye on them. It was the inherent gravitas of his office that was supposed to protect their honor and dignity.

The girls put the glass windows to good use. They took turns standing by them and stealing clandestine glances at the players. At any given time, only two or three of the girls enjoyed this privilege because the rest were planted in various parts of the room to ensure that neither the headmaster nor any other teacher might walk in suddenly and catch them in the act.

The system worked well. Usually. It had only one structural flaw. What if more than one girl liked the same boy? The first time they realized the windows were not wide enough was when jealousy made its inroad and a quarrel broke out. They couldn't decide who should have viewing rights, so that day the windows just stood there— clear, pristine, and useless—mocking the girls, their helplessness, and their inability to compromise.

These days, Fatehabad High School has nearly as many girls as boys. And from the outside, the headmaster's office does not seem as huge as it still is in my grandmother's memory. An ochre-colored wood plaque hangs from the door. It says "Headmaster" in Bengali. This door that bears countless prints of my grandmother's hands, feels cool and damp to touch. I count the reasons that brought her to this room—the promise of safety, the jubilation of prizes and congratulations, maybe a punishment or two.

I imagine my grandmother as a teenager walking down this corridor with other girls her age. They are escorted by a straight-backed, strict-looking male teacher. Her small-slim frame is wrapped in a starched cotton sari. Her hair is parted in the middle and woven into two braids with ribbons tied at the end. From her right shoulder, hangs a cotton bag stacked with newspaper-wrapped books, notebooks, pencils, and fountain pens. Her hands are by her sides as behooves a young woman of her status. She knocks politely on the headmaster's door and when she enters, she glances at the windows to see if a football match is going on.

I turn away in search of my uncle. Without a gaggle of teenage faces pressed against them, the windows look just as they once did—clear, pristine, and useless.

৳০

I'm on my way back to India and from there to Idaho. I have filled two journals, clicked over a thousand photographs. In the immigration line, I am miraculously face-to-face with the same customs officer who interviewed me when I first entered the country. We greet each other like long-lost family members. "How was Fatehabad?" he asks.

I am taken aback. He must interview hundreds of people every day. "How did you even remember where I was headed?"

He waves aside my incredulity and gives me another tobacco-stained smile. "There aren't too many people who come here from Moscow, Idaho, via Calcutta, India, for Fatehabad, Bangladesh."

I have to laugh. "Fatehabad was perfect. Your country is beautiful."

"It's yours, too. Please visit again."

I know I will. A bit of Bangladesh has permanently become mine. Back in Idaho, every time I eat a pan-seared salmon, my mouth will hunger for my aunt's hot and spicy shutki. I will never forget how I devoured the crunchy briny fish for lunch as well as dinner, though it set my tongue on fire and stained my nails yellow. I will miss the soothing evening breeze of the Chittagong harbor and the local insistence on adding salt to lemon-based soda drinks to increase their tanginess. I will miss seeing the angular letters of the Bengali script everywhere. It took Bangladesh to make me realize that the letters are interwoven in my spine. I will miss the warmth and hospitality of my family there, the solidity of our shared history, and the thrill of uncovering all that can still tie us together.

But I will not miss the stares, the way pedestrians stopped in their strides to watch me take photographs. I will not miss being one of the few women on the streets nor the odd gift and bind it was to be chaperoned.

The memory I want to clench in my hands,

however, has nothing to do with land or nationality. It bears no connection to my ancestral home or to my grandparents or their stories that compelled me to seek mine. Instead, it's about a four-year-old boy whose mother is a distant cousin. She is a Hindu and her husband, a Muslim. Five years ago when they fell in love and got married, their families combusted with rage and disappointment. It was hard to tell which set of parents felt more betrayed. They were united in their disavowal of the Hindu bride and the Muslim groom, until the birth of their son. That mended the broken relationships. Now the grandson spends time with both sets of grandparents. He joyously celebrates Id and Diwali, and says profound sentences like, "Ya Allah, tomorrow we will go to the Kali Temple, and after that, eat two ice creams." It's the best of both worlds, this story, rich with sweetness and hope, where Allah and Kali coexist. This, I will grab in my fists. This, I won't let go.

Oscillation

I.

When I was nine years old, I read *Swiss Family Robinson*, and it exploded my imagination. My family and I lived in a middle-class neighborhood in New Delhi, the capital city of India, far, far removed from the social and cultural milieu of early 19th century Switzerland in which Johann Wyss wrote his masterpiece. Sure, our overcrowded city was distant from every shoreline, but that didn't stop me from imagining my family sailing on a huge ship and crashing (gently) onto an uninhabited island. I took it for granted that once there, like the Robinsons, my family, too, would get into fierce adventures with an impossible array of wild animals. We would grow our own food, collect dazzling pearls, and transform a hollowed out cave into our home. Most importantly, I would have a magnificent treehouse to disappear to every afternoon with an enormous stash of books.

The evening I finished reading *Swiss Family Robinson*, I decided that it would be appropriate to share my plans for our future over dinner. It didn't occur to me that neither of my city-bred parents had ever touched an animal that hadn't been brought home from our local butcher shop or that, for most of their lives, they had lived in apartments. I enunciated my plan over fish curry and rice. Ma nodded, but I could see from the way she concentrated on picking out the bones that she wasn't totally sold on the idea. Clearly, she would need more persuading. Baba, on the other hand, ate in his usual brisk manner, but maintained eye contact throughout. Good. I had his complete attention. He heard me out but brought up a practical problem: "All of the world's surface area has already been mapped," he said, "There isn't anything left to be discovered. Where will we go?" His question stumped me. I knew he had to be right. He was always right. This was beyond disappointing, but I appreciated his honesty and was relieved we had figured this out before actually boarding the ship. His final words on the topic, however, cheered me up.

"You can have an adventure any time you want," he said. "All you need is your imagination and the willingness to step out."

II.

Years passed, we continued to live in New Delhi, and I swiftly came to realize how imperative it was that girls and women in my city not have a sense of adventure at all. Venturing anywhere outside our immediate neighborhood, even if it were a short walk across the street to buy candy, could elicit catcalls, whistles, and unwanted invitations. Bus rides were the worst. If unfortunate enough to be standing, a stray hand could reach out from anywhere to pinch, poke, stroke, or cop a feel. If sitting down, the nearest man could mistake your arm as a platform to rub himself.

I learned the name of this peculiar brand of behavior: *Eve-teasing*, a term prevalent all over South Asia. Its biblical connotations are curious given that Christians and Jews together comprise a minority in our part of the world. Irrespective of religious differences, the implication is clear: It is always the woman's fault. It is the temptress in us, in all of our collective DNA beginning with Eve, which leads men astray.

Which is why Eve-teasing is a part of any Indian woman's life. It can sneak up on you in crowded public places and isn't dependent on secret alleyways or red-light districts. It doesn't require women to be urban or rural, to dress conservatively or provocatively, to be a teenager or significantly older. In a country divided on caste and class distinctions, Eve-teasing is the great equalizer.

Worse, it comes stamped with an inbuilt sense of machismo, a kind of bravado that is lent its normalcy by our cinema, especially the Hindi film industry, popularly called Bollywood. For the longest time, in film after film, the entire courtship period between the boy and girl would begin when the boy spotted the girl, and immediately thereafter, he and his friends would begin to tease her. Sure, she would huff and puff, but it wasn't real rage. It was indignation, and it was cute, because like a small child, she didn't know any better. She hadn't yet been tamed of her wild ways. Whereas the boy already knew what was good for her, for him, and for the two of them together, so he would persist and eventually win her over—his rightful prize, the ever-dutiful, modest, Indian bride.

III.

The Hindi phrase for rape is *izzat lutna*. Literally translated, it means "stealing honor." As a child, I heard the phrase in movies and TV shows, and because for the most part, Indian media was extremely conservative, all they ever showed was a woman being pounced upon by a man. I assumed it to mean beating, clearly a terrible thing to do to anyone defenseless, irrespective of gender. But the "stealing honor" part never made sense. When a man roughed up another man, of which there were several instances in cinema, why didn't the victim say he had lost honor? Why was it only applicable in the case of women? And why was it that afterward these dishonored women on screen were allowed only one of three options: embrace a life of recrimination and indignity, commit suicide, or marry the rapist, as if a lifetime with someone bestial could somehow turn magical?

IV.

But what about the other end of the spectrum? What if the option of marriage itself was denied? The way it was 400 years ago in the court of the mighty Mughal emperor, Shah Jahan. He established a fine city and in the manner of all megalomaniacal rulers everywhere, named it after himself: Shahjahanabad, the City of Shah Jahan. It was a walled wealthy conclave with fourteen gates that guards locked up at night. Shah Jahan, a man of many accomplishments, including building the Taj Mahal, is popularly thought of as a great romantic. After all, he did build the world's grandest and most beautiful mausoleum for his principal wife, and for as long as she was alive, he is reputed to have been monogamous, a rare feat for any medieval ruler.

But it is this very same sensitive, romantic man who passed a curious decree soon after wearing the crown of the emperor: He forbade his own daughters and nieces from marrying. He believed their marriage would diminish the pride of the royal family, for how could the princesses ever find grooms of a stature higher than theirs? Plus, there was the additional concern their marriages would increase the number of aspirants to the throne.

I imagine the scene inside the Mughal harem that particular afternoon. I imagine the oldest princess, Jahanara, already established as a formidable poet and philanthropist, immersed in a new Persian verse. I imagine her younger sisters and cousins tightly knotted into a group, gossiping away from her, breaking into peals of laughter like teenage girls everywhere. And then, the arrival of the palace eunuchs bearing a royal decree. Probably the girls ignored them at first. They were used to the eunuchs, those adult men castrated in their boyhood but entrusted to protect the harem from the world outside that quivered like a mirage, laden with temptations.

I imagine their leader summoned the princesses to the courtyard, gave them the briefest of glances, and then read out the decree, carefully keeping his eyes locked to the page. How did the princesses react? Did they rush to their rooms, their anklets and bracelets cantankerous and irritable, echoing with every ounce of their being as they willed the decree to be a joke, even though in their hearts they knew emperors are not prone to humor? Did they collapse onto each other sobbing for support, wiping tears with the expensive gossamer muslins from Bengal, which they so favored? Did someone faint from shock while others resisted the urge to misbehave, if only for this one time in their entire lives, and to experience that excruciating thrill that comes from hurling a heavy vase against a full-length mirror, watching it crumble into a thousand fragments of stardust? Or were they quiet and solemn as they buried dreams that featured a husband and a brood of children, reconciling themselves to a life caged within the same four walls of the harem that would see them from childhood to deathbed?

And through their grief, did they curse the man behind the decree—Shah Jahan, their emperor, father to some, uncle to others? How could a man so wedded to romance be this cruel to his own daughters and nieces? Why deny them their opportunity for happiness when they had grown up in his shadow, watching him wrestle with the agony that comes from losing one's beloved?

V.

These days, Shahjahanbad is a maze of noisy traffic, narrow streets, and an endless wave of people. But on Sundays, a portion of it transforms into a secondhand book bazaar. Makeshift stalls and booksellers sprout as if by magic from the ancient sidewalks. The bazaar attracts readers and collectors from all over the city and for those blessed hours, we sift through books worn and new, literary and scientific, under the watchful gaze of old buildings.

The book bazaar was one of my favorite haunts as a college student. Sometimes, I went with friends, but mostly I went by myself and spent nearly all the money I had managed to beg, borrow, and earn throughout the month.

It was a Sunday in March of 2002, and after having spent the entire afternoon buying books, I was left with only a handful of rupees and knew it was time to return home. The bus stop was mostly empty, but it smelled faintly of onions, old socks, and body odor. I didn't care; I had a backpack full of new books.

When my bus arrived, I found a seat fairly easily. What made it even better was that I had it all to myself. I leaned back, my arm wrapped protectively around my backpack, the two of us quiet and content against the snarls of New Delhi's impatient traffic. I sat up straighter when there was less than a kilometer to my home, which was also the last stop for the bus. I realized I was the only woman on board; there were three other passengers who sat separately, looking out their respective windows, minding their business, just as I was minding mine.

I confirmed the last stop with the conductor, a small mousy man with a pronounced squint and heaved on my backpack, about to stand up. But instead of slowing down, the bus picked up speed. I could tell it was headed towards a remote stretch of Delhi's greenbelt known as Jahanpanah Forest.

From the corner of my eye, I saw those three passengers rise from their respective seats and slide on to those in front of me. I gripped the handlebar, struggling to keep my expression neutral. They began talking to each other animatedly, and I listened to them, to the matter-of-fact way they discussed what they were going to do to me as if I weren't there, as if I were a dumb animal that wouldn't understand their words or intent. I realized they were friends, not just with each other but also with the driver and the conductor. They had probably decided I was the entertainment for their evening the moment I purchased my ticket and informed the conductor I would be getting off at the very last stop.

I glanced at the closed door and windows. It was a busy evening in Delhi, but no one would ever hear my screams, and even if they did, few would probably jump in to help a stranger. I knew my city well. And so did they, which is what boosted their confidence. Within minutes, I would be in Jahanpanah Forest, an unforgiving landscape heavy with thorny trees.

Just then, I felt the bus slowing down. We had caught the very end of a traffic light. It was orange for a second before flicking to green, and I had that moment within which to make up my mind: Stay inside the bus and embrace whatever fate lay ahead or jump, knowing the massive tires of the bus would be mere inches from my legs.

I gripped my backpack and swung it over my shoulders. There wasn't any time to lose, to pause, or think. I ran to the heavy door and pushed it open. I shot a quick glance at the men. They sat immobile, pasted to the seats as if from shock, their eyes widened at my stupidity. Even though it was clear I was going to jump, none of them tried to pull me back. I knew what that meant: If not me, there would be someone else. There is no dearth of young vulnerable women in a large city.

I jumped, broke into a run, the tires barely a foot or so away from me, and didn't stop until I reached home.

VI.

In August of 2006, I left Delhi for an adventure abroad. My destination: Moscow, Idaho. I enrolled at the University of Idaho to fulfill a lifelong dream to study writing. On my first day, my roommate, a doctoral student of biology, who had arrived from India a year ago, gave me an unofficial tour. I was bowled over by the green-leafy gorgeousness of the campus, by the overall systematic cleanliness, by the friendliness and ease with which everyone seemed to go about in Moscow, my new hometown with a population of less than 25,000. I was comforted by the red-brick architecture of the building that housed the English Department. Perhaps the fact that both my undergrad and grad degrees in India had been from red-brick institutions had something to do with it. But knowing appearances can deceive, I asked my roommate, "How safe do you feel here?"

She answered without a moment's hesitation, "I often walk back home from my lab past midnight. All I need is my phone to feel safe."

Her words reassured me, but they weren't enough, and so during our first week, I bombarded her with questions, such as, "Can I just go outside and lie on the grass and read a book? Nothing will happen? No Eve-teasing?"

Someone else might have found my questions weird or strange but not her. She had spent many summers in Delhi. She only said, "You will be fine."

The following summer, one of my American friends from the creative writing program invited me and another of our classmates to visit her hometown in north Idaho. We set out for our three-day trip, driving on mountain roads lush with tall Douglas firs. It was a kind of green very different from the tropical one I had known back home. It was somehow more aloof and somber with temperatures perfect for picnics—warm and inviting during the day but deliciously chilly at night. When we pulled into the driveway, I saw the mere handful of houses that made up the entire village and felt a tiny frisson of sadness for my friend, for the reality of having to grow up in a world so small, so inward looking, so far away from the giddying choices of cinemas, theaters, museums, bookstores, and restaurants I had taken for granted all my life in New Delhi.

The following day, my friend took us to a river beach that her family had frequented since she was a little girl. It was quiet and peaceful, save for the wind whooshing through the trees, the gurgle and ripple of the water—its surface so clear the pebbles shone like jewels—and the complete absence of traffic. The three of us were alone on the beach and my American friends decided to go skinny-dipping, a term I had only vaguely encountered in books. Within seconds, however, they demonstrated what it actually meant and to my absolute horror, I was now face-to-face with two adult, naked, white women—a form of human life I had previously encountered only in cinema. They plunged themselves into the cold water, giggling with excitement and at my stunned expression.

I watched them from the shore, my toes buried in sand, jeans rolled up to my knees, and my nerves knotted up with anxiety, fear, and embarrassment. At that moment, our gender was our only commonality, and I felt distant from them as if our friendship and passion for books and writing had been peeled and cast aside, just like their clothes. There could not be a starker reminder of the difference between my world and theirs in terms of nationality, culture, and definition of modesty. It reiterated what I already knew about myself: I would never feel their level of comfort or safety in any part of the world, no matter how small or inward-looking because my Indian-ness would never take a backseat and allow me to be as uninhibited as them. I also wondered, with a touch of envy, how it might have been to grow up in a small town in north Idaho, surrounded by lofty forests, a sparse population, and a very different kind of freedom than I had ever known.

VII.

On Sunday, December 16, 2012, I was very much in Moscow. I don't remember the specifics of what I did the entire day, but I imagine it was like most other Sundays: I woke up on my own without an alarm clock blaring in the background and slowly made my way to the kitchen, where I made a big breakfast and coffee while listening to music. I went grocery shopping in the afternoon and returned with ingredients for a stew. I tossed it all into the slow-cooker, looking forward to its simmering goodness for dinner.

Halfway across the world in Delhi, a twenty-three-year-old woman and her male friend watched the movie *Life of Pi* at a theater. I wonder if she loved it as much as I did. I imagine she and her friend were still talking about the film—its music, the lyrical imagery, the special effects that made the tiger, Richard Parker, come alive—as they walked to the nearest bus stop. Within minutes, a bus pulled in, looking just as ordinary as the hundreds of others that crisscross Delhi's labyrinth of roads every day. The young woman and her friend checked with the conductor. Yes, the bus was headed in the direction of their home, and they hopped on board.

What was the first thing she did? Scan around for a good seat? Probably not near the windows. December is a chilly unforgiving month in Delhi. Did she even glance at the four men pretending to be co-passengers? I assume she didn't, lost as she may have been still discussing *Life of Pi*, grateful as she must have been to be out of the cold, heading toward the warm cocoon of her home.

But how swiftly did the mood inside the bus change? At what point did it dawn on her that this was not going to end well, that the four passengers, the driver, and the conductor were all friends? Was it when they pinned her down? When they started beating her friend with an iron rod? Or when they decided to use it on her again and again and again as an additional weapon of sexual assault?

I learned about it the next morning while reading *The Times of India* through the convenient app on my phone, from the warmth and safety of my bed in Moscow. Numbly, I called home. My parents refused to talk about it. Ma's reaction was clear and emphatic. She had skimmed the headlines and that was it. She would not read the details of a rape conducted inside a moving bus. Her last words on the topic were, "You were twenty-two. She is twenty-three."

VIII.

Whether I talk to my mother on the phone or via Skype, one of her questions remains the same: "How much longer will you live so far away?"

Most days, I hastily change the topic. I ask about our neighbors or distract her by pretending to be one of our annoying relatives until she bursts into giggles. But other days, I am not as nimble, and Ma catches on to my hesitation and homesickness. "Come back to Delhi," she insists, "Come back to us. There are excellent opportunities here."

I promise to look into it. And I do. Half-heartedly. I tell her my reasons: "I don't want to return to a world where I will hesitate to travel by myself, where if I go out to eat on my own or buy a drink, someone will assume that I am asking for it. All I want is a little bit of dignity."

My voice cracks with frustration. I know the comparisons are unfair: Delhi is approximately 90 times the physical size of Moscow; its population 600 times greater. I thank Ma silently for not stating the obvious, while I hide from her how some nights I lie awake, oscillating between gratitude and fear: I have never been in a serious accident, never broken a bone, never been hospitalized. What if someday something terrible happens to compensate for all this good fortune, something so terrible that my parents never see me alive? Worse, what if something happens to them, and I can't make it there on time?

This time, it is Ma who changes the subject.

IX.

I am constantly haunted by the image of Shah Jahan's daughters. I imagine they gathered in secret the night they first heard his punishing decree. Maybe they met inside the chamber of the youngest princess, after carefully posting their maids in attendance, so they would be alerted in case a patrolling eunuch was around.

I wonder if they cursed us, all of us future girls and women of Delhi, and bequeathed to us this life of constant oscillation between guilt and fear, just so the world will grant us our sliver of peace and dignity. Are we echoing their dilemma in having to choose between our duties toward families and our desires as young women?

It's a difficult choice, this dice I roll inside my head every day. Is it better to return to Delhi, where I can once again embrace my nationality, seep into its rich history and the many, many exotic offerings of food, art and cinema, the sheer choices that come with living in a huge city, even if it means needing a male companion to travel with at night, and tutoring my senses so I no longer hear catcalls nor feel the touch of an intrusive roving hand? Or is it better to live on in this tiny university town so far away from India, from the people and culture that define me, where I have to explain and defend where I come from, but where I can enter a restaurant by myself to enjoy a glass of wine without raising eyebrows, and then walk back home late at night, my mobility as a woman not dependent on anyone else?

I will myself to return to my present: a Saturday morning inside my apartment, quiet, save for the familiar gurgle of my coffeemaker. From the living room window, I see the neighbor's red and yellow tulips in full bloom. The parking lot is crammed, a telltale sign that this is graduation weekend, and proud parents have poured into town to celebrate their sons and daughters. I imagine the happy faces and wish my parents lived across the street, instead of halfway around the world.

I sit down at the dining table to finish making my grocery list for the coming week. Besides basics like milk and coffee, I include ingredients for a Mexican chicken soup and Thai fried rice. At age nine, I wanted an island adventure replete with a tree house—my family and exotic animals for company. Now, in my thirties, with a full-time job and other responsibilities, my most frequent adventures take the form of gastronomic experiments inside my kitchen, for I have also discovered the comforts of being a creature of habit.

The microwave clock tells me it is 9 a.m., meaning 9:30 p.m. in India. It's time for my weekend call to my parents. The phone rings twice, and Baba answers. The first time I heard his voice after coming to America, I burst into tears. He kept saying "Hello" and repeating my name, but I clamped a hand tightly over my mouth, refusing to let him hear the homesickness, the loneliness, and the request, "Baba, will you please come here and pick me up?"

Right now, though, Baba tells me they are just finishing dinner. I ask if I should call later. My father, the most considerate man in the world, pooh-poohs my question. We make small talk. When we are physically face-to-face, he and I can chat for hours—history, politics, geography, books, personal stories—but the phone makes us reserved and awkward. Still we persist, until Ma is done with dinner and can come to the phone.

My coffeemaker beeps. I grab the largest mug I own and fill it to the brim. I settle down, put up my feet, and dig into the cookie jar. This conversation will last only for an hour or two, but it will nourish me for days. For now, that is all I need.

Born in Calcutta and raised in New Delhi, Sayantani Dasgupta teaches at the University of Idaho. Her essays and stories have appeared in *The Rumpus*, *Phoebe*, and *Gulf Stream*, among other magazines and literary journals. She edits nonfiction for *Crab Creek Review*, and previous honors include a Pushcart Prize Special Mention and a Centrum Fellowship. In *Fire Girl*, her debut collection of essays, Sayantani examines her personal story against the history, religion, popular culture and mythology of South Asia and her current home in the American West. To learn more about Sayantani, visit: www.sdasgupta.com

Publications by Two Sylvias Press:

The Daily Poet: Day-By-Day Prompts For Your Writing Practice
by Kelli Russell Agodon and Martha Silano (Print and eBook)

The Daily Poet Companion Journal (Print)

Fire On Her Tongue:
An Anthology of Contemporary Women's Poetry
edited by Kelli Russell Agodon and Annette Spaulding-Convy
(Print and eBook)

The Poet Tarot and Guidebook: A Deck Of Creative Exploration
(Print and App)

Fire Girl: Essays on India, America, and the In-Between
by Sayantani Dasgupta (Print and eBook)

Naming The No-Name Woman,
Winner of the 2015 Two Sylvias Press Chapbook Prize
by Jasmine An (Print and eBook)

Blood Song
by Michael Schmeltzer (Print and eBook)

Phantom Son
by Sharon Estill Taylor (Print and eBook)

Community Chest
by Natalie Serber (Print)

What The Truth Tastes Like
by Martha Silano (Print and eBook)

landscape/heartbreak
by Michelle Peñaloza (Print and eBook)

Earth, Winner of the 2014 Two Sylvias Press Chapbook Prize
by Cecilia Woloch (Print and eBook)

The Cardiologist's Daughter
by Natasha Kochicheril Moni (Print and eBook)

She Returns to the Floating World
by Jeannine Hall Gailey (Print and eBook)

The Two Sylvias Press Journalette Series
(Blank Journals)

Hourglass Museum
by Kelli Russell Agodon (eBook only)

Cloud Pharmacy
by Susan Rich (eBook only)

Dear Alzheimer's: A Caregiver's Diary & Poems
by Esther Altshul Helfgott (eBook only)

Listening to Mozart: Poems of Alzheimer's
by Esther Altshul Helfgott (eBook only)

Crab Creek Review 30th Anniversary Issue featuring Northwest Poets
edited by Kelli Russell Agodon and Annette Spaulding-Convy
(Print and eBook)

Please visit Two Sylvias Press (www.twosylviaspress.com) for information on purchasing our print books, eBooks, writing tools, and for submission guidelines for our annual chapbook prize. Two Sylvias Press also offers editing services and manuscript consultations.

For creative inspiration and writing news, sign up for the Two Sylvias Press Newsletter: www.tinyletter.com/twosylviaspress

**Created with the belief
that great writing is good for the world.**

two sylvias press

Visit us online: www.twosylviaspress.com